Miraculously My Own

Joyce Grammer Lacey

Miraculously My Own
Trilogy Christian Publishers A Wholly Owned Subsidiary of Trinity Broadcasting Network
2442 Michelle Drive Tustin, CA 92780
Copyright © 2021 by Joyce Lacey
Scripture quotations marked AMP are taken from the Amplified® Bible (AMP), Copyright © 2015 by The Lockman Foundation. Used by permission. www.Lockman.org.
Scripture quotations marked HCSB are taken from the Holman Christian Standard Bible®, Used by Permission HCSB ©1999, 2000, 2003, 2009 Holman Bible Publishers. Holman Christian Standard Bible®, Holman CSB®, and HCSB® are federally registered trademarks of Holman Bible Publishers.
Scripture quotations marked MSG are taken from THE MESSAGE, copyright © 1993, 2002, 2018 by Eugene H. Peterson. Used by permission of NavPress. All rights reserved. Represented by Tyndale House Publishers, Inc.
Scripture quotations marked NASB are taken from the New American Standard Bible® (NASB), Copyright © 1960, 1962, 1963, 1968, 1971, 1972, 1973, 1975, 1977, 1995 by The Lockman Foundation. Used by permission. www.Lockman.org.
Scripture quotations marked NIV are taken from the Holy Bible, New International Version®, NIV®. Copyright © 1973, 1978, 1984, 2011 by Biblica, Inc.™ Used by permission of Zondervan. All rights reserved worldwide. www.zondervan.com. The "NIV" and "New International Version" are trademarks registered in the United States Patent and Trademark Office by Biblica, Inc.™
Scripture quotations marked NKJV are taken from the New King James Version®. Copyright © 1982 by Thomas Nelson. Used by permission. All rights reserved.
Scripture quotations marked KJV are taken from the King James Version of the Bible. Public domain.
No part of this book may be reproduced, stored in a retrieval system, or transmitted by any means without written permission from the author. All rights reserved. Printed in the USA.
Rights Department, 2442 Michelle Drive, Tustin, CA 92780.
Trilogy Christian Publishing/TBN and colophon are trademarks of Trinity Broadcasting Network.
For information about special discounts for bulk purchases, please contact Trilogy Christian Publishing.
Trilogy Disclaimer: The views and content expressed in this book are those of the author and may not necessarily reflect the views and doctrine of Trilogy Christian Publishing or the Trinity Broadcasting Network.
Manufactured in the United States of America
10 9 8 7 6 5 4 3 2 1
Library of Congress Cataloging-in-Publication Data is available.
ISBN: 978-1-63769-196-0
E-ISBN: 978-1-63769-197-7

Adoption Creed

"Not flesh of my flesh\or bone of my bone, still miraculously my own.

Never forget for a single minute,
you did not grow under my heart but in it."

By: Fleur Conkling Heyleger

Miraculously My Own

Dedicated to my precious family, who were my inspirations to write this book.

Especially Todd, who taught us all how to love unconditionally through his life of turmoil.

Foreword

God has had His hand on Joyce's life from birth to this day. Everyone who meets and/or talks with her sees the joy she has both for the Lord and for people.

Her laugh and smile are infectious, and she will lift your spirit to new heights. She knows and understands the love of God, Jesus, and the Holy Spirit.

I know that you will enjoy and better understand the Trinity after reading her writings.

I'm most blessed, for you see, I am her husband.

Larry Lacey

Acknowledgements

First and foremost, I want to thank my son, Todd, who allowed me to write about his life. It is his desire, as well as mine, that many will benefit from his life story.

Larry, the greatest husband in the world, has been very patient as I sought to hear from God. Though I spent many hours, he never complained or in any way discouraged me.

My daughter, Jill, encouraged me to add a study guide, which I redid as a workbook to help people learn the Word of God concerning parenting.

Thank you to Jill's husband, Mick, for sharing Jill in the preparation of the manuscript.

To Trent, my youngest son, who always encourages and supports us. I thank him specifically, for setting up and helping me with a computer.

Jackie (Trent's wife) was also a great help. She did some typing for the manuscript, and helped me when I got stuck on the computer. She is always a willing participant in any family project.

To my niece, Patti Jo (Luizzo) McCreanor, who provided the poems on adoption that touched the heart.

God made it possible for me to become acquainted with Anita Williams, a psycho-therapist and a wonderful Christian lady. Though we attended the same class in high school, we never met until recently. Anita supplied me with

Miraculously My Own

invaluable statistical information on adoption issues.

I also want to thank Carma Naylor, who has just written a book and has come to my rescue on how to get a book ready to be published.

Also, a big "thank you" goes to Barbara Wiggins. A dear friend and brilliant lady, who helped type my "original" manuscript. And now, she is with the Lord.

To Deborah Hill and her daughter, Kaitlyn, who helped me organize the chapters on the computer and put them on a disc. Deborah also graciously offered to edit the book

Much appreciation goes to Diane Mierzwik, author and owner of The Writer's Gallery in Yucaipa, and a former Bible student of mine. Diane edited the *Miraculously My Own Workbook* that accompanies this book. Diane also taught me computer techniques that would help in publishing the *Miraculously My Own* book, workbook, and prayer journal. Her Writer's Gallery critique group critiqued my book and workbook, and they were an incredible encouragement to me even when tough on me. They taught me humility and how to write from the reader's point of view. Thanks, gang!

Mary Gauer taught me how to listen and hear from God. Without understanding how to hear God's voice, I could not and would not have been able to write this book.

I also want to thank Irmgart Mitchell, my new neighbor who helped me as I struggled with my lack of computer skills and also typed two chapters that had somehow gotten

Acknowledgements

deleted. She also helped me to correctly insert the pictures I wanted in this book.

Above all else, I want to express my deep gratitude to my Abba Father in heaven who put the desire in my heart to write about our son, Todd, and the urgent need to share our story with other parents.

My Lord Jesus Christ, who wants to save me from the struggles that I encounter in life by sending me His Holy Spirit as a comforter and guide.

The Holy Spirit, who never gave up on me when I was not sure where, when, how, or if I could ever make this project a reality. He just kept showing me a step at a time how and what I was to do next. I praise and thank You, Father, Son, and Holy Spirit!

Introduction

When I began writing this story about Todd, our adopted, special needs son, I had no specific plan. I just felt compelled to write. It did cross my mind that my family might read it and get some understanding of the struggle we had to keep ahead of Satan's onslaughts. I knew Satan came to steal, kill, and destroy. He almost succeeded and would have in all three areas had it not been for the faithfulness of our Father in heaven.

When trials and test came our way, God helped my husband, Larry, and me through them. He directed us as we were willing to listen. He desired to listen to our pain and shorten our trials. All broken relationships, tragedies, chaos, are the result of our fallen world and they are *not* God's will, though He does use them to help us mature.

I wanted to share what God put on my heart through the Holy Spirit so parents who have never heard any prompting from the Holy Spirit will realize that He has actually been speaking to them all along.

There are thoughts and scriptures that helped my husband and me to open our ears and hearts so we could hear, begin to fight the good fight of faith, and win the battles we faced daily.

There are times we believe that we are the only ones with our particular problem; therefore, we feel alone. However, I Corinthians, 10: 13 is a scripture to help us know that we are *not* alone. It says:

> *No temptation (trial or test) has overtaken you but such as common to man, and God is faithful Who will not allow you to be tempted beyond what youare able, but with the temptation will provide the wayof escape also, that you may be able to endure it.*
>
> — I Corinthians 10: 13, NASB

God does not *fix* every trial we are going through. There are times we *need* to go through a test or trial. Our spiritual *eyes will open and we will see* God's hand as He gladly gives us the victory. We are then *qualified* to help someone else who is going through a similar ordeal, and we can comfort them, and they will know they are not alone.

God wants each of us to walk through life receiving His peace and joy in the midst of trials. As *"more than conquerors,"* He then tells us to help and comfort one another (II Corinthians, 1:3-4, NKJV).

The desire of my heart is for this book to help *all* parents, especially adoptive parents, and parents of special needs children to know the importance of drawing close to God and listening to His Spirit. Then He draws close and answers the prayers and cries of our heart (James 4: 8). Also, we begin to recognize Satan's subtle ways, how he works through us, our children, other family members, and

Introduction

sometimes even our friends to cause division and chaos in our homes and our lives.

Come along with Larry and me and discover this peace for yourself. God will bless you and guide you by His Spirit as we travel.

During this journey, our family found the peace that we so desperately needed. It was peace that only Jesus the "Prince of Peace" could give.

TABLE OF CONTENTS

Chapter 1 21
Once Upon a Time

Chapter 2 31
We Want a Baby, God! Important Information About Adoption

Chapter 3 47
"Happy Dazes"

Chapter 4 55
The Teen Years

Chapter 5 69
Unconditional Love

Chapter 6 81
Friends – Better Than a "Shrink!"

Chapter 7 93
Discovering the "Abba" Father

Chapter 8 103
Dark Forces of Evil

Chapter 9 121
More Years of Trial

Chapter 10 125
Perseverance and Endurance Under Trial (a Love Producer)

Chapter 11 135
Effectual Prayer

Chapter 12 151
The Loving Act of Discipline

Chapter 13 159
Why Praise?

Chapter 14 171
Growing in My Faith

Chapter 15 181
Abiding in Love (The "Perfect Peace" Puzzle)

Chapter 16 187
Todd's Story - Growing Up as an Adopted
Child with a Disability

Chapter 17 201
Peace at Last – "Happily Ever After"
Because of "Prince" Jesus

Purpose

It is my desire that all parents--particularly *adoptive* parents and parents of *special needs* children--will see the importance of listening for the guidance of the Holy Spirit while in the process of raising their children.

I see this book and all that it may accomplish as a blessing and a reward for all the trials we encountered. God, as He says in His Word, has made something good out of the difficult times we as Todd's parents experienced while on our parenting journey.

To God be the glory!

Miraculously My Own book, workbook and prayer journal will be available for both church classes and home Bible studies, and it will inspire parents, especially those who are struggling to raise a special needs child.

Chapter 1

"ONCE UPON A TIME"

*For I know the plans I have for you, declares the Lord, plans to prosper you **And** not to harm you, plans to give you a hope and a future.*

— Jeremiah 29: 11, NIV

There once was a little girl and a little boy who should have met years before they did. The little boy lived right behind the little girl and attended the same grade school, and they were in the same grade but were not in the same classroom.

The little girl lived across the street from the park. It was where she played because she and her family lived in a tiny apartment with no yard. The little boy played at that park too. The girl frequented the wading pool at the park, as did the boy. She painted in the little ceramic shop for children. He did too. Every year at the park, she attended the annual barbeque that he always did too. At the end of summer, the park also had a watermelon feed, and they both were there. Did they ever bump into each other while enjoying any of those activities at the park? No, they did not.

After second grade, the boy, Larry, and his family

Miraculously My Own

moved across town, and Larry attended school there--third thru eighth grade.

While still in grade school, my friend since kindergarten Kay Kiker and I joined the Knot Hole Club for kids who wanted to cheer for the high school football team.

Kay had a friend named Wynn. He and his friends sat right behind us and were always teasing us and pulling our hair as boys like to do.

My father died when I was eleven. My mom, sister, and I moved to Buena Park. I

joined Job's Daughters, and this boy, Larry, was in DeMolay. These organizations had dances and other get-togethers. Did we meet then? No, it was not yet the right time.

The summer between eighth grade and high school, Larry moved to Buena Park, right next door to my best friend at the time. She told me all about this "cute" boy who moved next door to her named Larry. She said sometimes he would go up on the sundeck at his house. So, we always tried to see him when I visited her. Did we ever see him? No! Her father owned the dime store in town, and Larry worked for him occasionally. I never saw him in the store when I was in there. Even though Larry and I lived only a few blocks from each other, we never met around town either.

At the end of our sophomore year, my girlfriend Lois

Rogers and I (we sang in duets and quartets together at church functions) were walking along at school and Lois turned and said, "Hi, Larry."

I said, "Hey, he's cute, who is he?"

Lois said, "Oh, that's Larry Lacey. I have typing with him. He's really a nice guy, want to meet him?"

I said, "Sure!"

The next recess Lois introduced me to Larry.

Another friend from church was having an ice cream party at her house, and Lois asked Larry if he would like to go with me.

He said, "Yes."

I was so excited, and after Larry left for class, I jumped up and down and said, "He can go, he can go!"

Our guardian angels must have been relieved of the "keeping us apart duty." I really don't know if that falls under the job description for guardian angels, but I do know when we did meet, it was the perfect time--God's time.

One day we were recounting our childhood. Larry or I happened to mention that we were in the kids' Knot Hole Club.

I said, "Wynn and his friends used to sit behind us and tease us and pull our hair!"

Larry said, "Oh yeah, I remember us doing that! Wynn was one of my best friends." Though we never met in the Knot Hole Club, Larry probably pulled my hair!

Our dating years were delightful. Larry was such a

gentleman, always doing things like opening the door for me, and when we attended school dances, without exception, he presented me with an orchid corsage to wear.

Senior Prom was at Disneyland theme park. In the early days, prom night was limited to just one school at a time. Everything was so beautiful--the girls in long gowns and the boys in tuxedos or white dinner jackets.

If you have been there at night, you know how beautiful the park is. Trees are all lit-up, and music is playing. It is what every young girl dreams it will be like when she begins dating a handsome "prince."

When Larry and I were seniors in high school, he took me to Hillcrest Park where there was a cross on a hill. He knelt down, proposed to me, and presented me with an engagement ring. How thrilled I was to say, "Yes!"

We also got to walk together at graduation. Larry and I dated three and a half years before we married, since both of us were only sixteen when we started dating.

Our wedding day, August 26, 1957, was so special. Larry worked for the Southern California Edison Co. and I worked over the summer and on weekends at The Chicken Dinner restaurant at Knott's Berry Farm. I also worked for a dentist just before we married. Knowing my mom's limited income, we were happy to pay for our wedding ourselves. However, Kelsey and Bertha owned a nursery, and they provided all the flowers as a gift.

ONCE UPON A TIME

Kelsey was like a second father to me. Kelsey had no children of his own and loved to take all the teenagers from church miniature golfing and to the drive-in restaurant for hamburgers and his favorite thing, deep dish, hot apple pie. I asked him if would walk me down the aisle on our wedding day. He said he'd be honored to do that.

I wished my father could have walked me down the aisle, but I believe God provided Kelsey to take his place.

Larry had signed up in the service for the Navy TAR program (Training and Administration of Reserves). Agreeing to the program meant he could stay in one place if he took an extra year. So, four months after our lovely wedding, we were sent to Seattle, Washington for three years.

We loved living in Seattle. Everything was so green. The beauty of the trees like the dogwood, the pink and white fruit trees that bloomed in the spring, and the flowers took my breath away. I especially enjoyed the purple, yellow, and many other colors of the iris and the gigantic (around twelve inches in diameter) chrysanthemums. All the flowers seemed larger in size than any I had seen of the same varieties in California.

While we were in Seattle, we discussed *our* plans for a family. We decided we would wait until the last year in the service to have our baby. We wanted a couple years to ourselves, but we also wanted the navy to deliver our baby because it would not cost us anything. We got our couple years and more.

Many years later, Larry and I learned that the Bible tells us that God can and does open and close the womb. There are biblical examples of both.

Example of God closing the womb:

In the Old Testament, (II Samuel 6:20-23, KJV) God closes the womb of Michal, David's wife, because she looks through the window and sees King David leaping and dancing before the Lord, and she despises him in her heart. Michal comes out to meet David and says, *"How glorious was the King of Israel today, who uncovered himself in the eyes of the handmaids of his servants"* (II Samuel 6:20, KJV). Because Michal criticizes David's manner of worshiping God, God closes her womb. As Christians, we need to be careful not to criticize other Christians' forms of worship. God is the only one qualified to accept or reject our worship.

God tells us in Heb. 13:8 (NASB) He is the same, *"Yesterday, today, and forever."*

Mal. 3: 6 (NASB) says, *"I the Lord do not change."* Therefore, God still opens and closes the womb. God says in Deut. 7: 12-13 that He blesses the fruit of the womb when we are obedient. Psalms 127:3 tells us children are a gift and a reward.

Someone might say, "How can that be? Think of all the babies born in the world. Some of those people don't even know God, so how could they be obedient and the baby be a reward from Him?" That is a fair question. The answer is that the Bible is a book *written to the people of God* and how He deals with them. God set up reproduction for all mankind. All babies are a gift but not all are a *reward* for *obedience*. Though a baby is a gift from God, many times they have to suffer the consequences of their ungodly parents.

The following is a Biblical example of God opening the womb:

God spoke to Abraham when he was seventy-five years old (Sarah was sixty-five) and told him He would make of him a great nation (Genesis 12: 2, 3).

Several years had passed since they heard the

unimaginable promise that they would have a son. They were still childless. So, Sarah decided to take matters into her own hands (Genesis 16:2). She told Abraham to sleep with her handmaid Hagar, to become a surrogate mother in order to fulfill God's promise. Hagar had a son by Abraham and named him Ishmael. Ishmael was not to be the covenant child. Sarah was to bear Abraham a son, and he was to be named Isaac (Genesis 17:19).

Gen. 18:1-9-15 (Translation from: Women of the Bible Devotional Study)

By: Ann Spangler & Jean E. Syswerda

"One day the Lord appeared to Abraham... while he was sitting at the entrance of his tent... v9) Where is your wife, Sarah? There in the tent, Abraham replied. Then the Lord said, I will surely return to you about this time next year and Sarah, will have a son.

Now Sarah who had been eavesdropping from inside the tent laughed and said, after I am worn out and my master is old will I now have this pleasure? But the Lord said to Abraham; why did Sarah Laugh and say, will I really have a child now that I am old? Is anything too hard for the Lord? I will return to you at the appointed time next year and Sarah will have a son. Because Sarah was afraid, she lied and said, I did not laugh. But he pressed her saying, yes, you did laugh."

Abraham was one hundred years old when Sarah, age ninety, gave birth to Isaac, whose name meant "laughter." Sarah said, *"God has brought me laughter, and everyone who hears about this will laugh with me"* (Genesis 21:6, NIV).

Larry and I were not aware that these scriptures could apply in any way to us. That we, like Sarah, were jumping ahead of God's plan and not trusting Him possibly to provide a different plan for our lives, especially since we had no fertility problem.

However, Larry and I did confidently know the Bible promises, *"God causes all things to work together for good to those who love God and are called according to his purpose"* (Rom. 8:28, NASB).

God knew our level of faith and lack of knowledge of the scriptures in regards to childbearing. Therefore, in His infinite love and mercy, God pre-arranged for us to adopt Todd exactly at the right time, for our sakes and for Todd's, though several years would pass before I realized or believed that last statement. I was sure many times that almost anyone would have been better parents for Todd than we were. It seemed everything we did backfired.

Miraculously My Own

Father,

Thank You for teaching us of your miraculous ways. Help us to believe in your mighty power and love for us.

In Jesus name,

Amen.

Chapter 2

WE WANT A BABY, GOD!

(Of Course, on *Our* Terms)

For you created my inmost being, you knit me together in my mother's womb. I praise you because I am fearfully and Wonderfully made; your works are wonderful; I know that full well.

— **Psalms 139: 13-14, NIV**

My husband and I, *modern thinkers* that we were, believed *we* were supposed to be in charge of our own lives, especially when it came to planning our family. During the first two years that we were in the military service, we took all the precautions known at the time.

The beginning of the third year, *we* decided *we* would have a baby. We said in effect, "Okay, God, *we* are ready now for a baby." (Psalms 127: 3-5, NASB) says, "Behold children are a gift of the Lord. The fruit of the womb is a reward!" Can you imagine telling a friend, "I'm ready now; you can give me a gift (specifying the gift)?" Then why did we think we could inform God when it was okay to give us a gift of a child? Yes, we could have prayed for a baby as a desire of our heart. God always wants us to communicate our desires to Him. Then trust Him to give us our desire, a baby, just at the right time.

We were saying, "Okay God, okay God," for one year, then two years, three years, eventually up to seven-and-a-half years, including the two *we* controlled! *We* decided God must have been too busy. We would just adopt a baby!

Todd was four weeks and five days old when we got Him from the adoption agency. He was so adorable. Long brown hair, so tiny, only 6 lbs., 13 oz. He had been in the care of a foster mother right from the hospital. She told us Todd had just gotten over jaundice that day.

WE WANT A BABY, GOD!

I'm Adopted!

I had a DREAM last night...
I had to choose a MOMMY and DADDY...
At first I wondered what to do...There were so many it seemed untrue...
Short, tall, thin and stout...
I couldn't decide which ones to pick out.
But I was as surprised as I could be...
My MOMMY and DADDY had already picked ME!!

Our Son

(Todd's picture super-imposed by permission by my niece, PattiJo Liuzzo McCreanor)

Miraculously My Own

The Legacy of an Adopted Child

*Once there were two women,
Who never knew each other,
One you do not remember.
The other you call MOTHER
Two different lives, shaped to make your one.
One became your guiding star.
The other became your sun.
The first gave you LIFE.
And the second taught you to live it.
The first gave you a need for love.
And the second was there to give it.
One gave you a nationality.
The other gave you a name.
One gave you a seed of talent.
The other gave you an aim.
One gave you emotions.
The other calmed your fears.
One gave you away; it was all she could do.
The other prayed for a child – and.
God led her straight to you.
And now you ask me, through your tears.
The age-old question unanswered through the years.
Heredity or environment, which are you the product of?
Neither my darling, neither.*

Just two differ kinds of LOVE.

--Author Unknown

WE WANT A BABY, GOD!

ADOPTION /FOSTER CHILD

I was just a thought
Not a whisper could I make
God looked down and saw
You had all that you could take.

He knew where I was,
No need to search the lands
He picked me up and kissed me
As he placed me in your hands.

This kiss will be remembered
Each time that you kiss me.
I know this kiss means love
Unconditionally, eternally.

If there is not a Heaven
Then how should I believe
That I came to be so blessed
With this family I received?

Crystal Dawn Perry

Though you were
born unto another
I was blessed enough
To become your mother.

Throughout my life
I'll cherish this role
For you have touched
My heart and soul.

Aparna Dyer

About a week after we brought Todd home, he started throwing up every time he ate. The pediatrician told us he had a projectile stomach. He said it doesn't show up until a few weeks after a baby is born. There is a little flap that sometimes doesn't develop as it should, and surgery could tack it down. Sometimes, it will develop on its own.

To prevent Todd from needing surgery, the doctor had me wrap him up tightly in a receiving blanket like a little papoose. Then he said to hold him very still for at least twenty to thirty minutes. After he ate, I lay him down on his right side with a pillow propped behind his back. At times, when he woke up, the crib would be soaked with vomit all around him; sometimes it even ran down on to the springs of the crib. It was a total wash-down many mornings and sometimes after naps. It was necessary to change Todd's clothes six to eight times a day. I loved dressing him though; he was so cute and really a very good baby. He managed to maintain enough weight and nutrition that surgery was not necessary. The projecting continued, slowly getting better until it stopped at eighteen months.

Todd's health was a constant challenge. He averaged a trip to the doctor's office about every other week for the first two years of his life. Some of the reasons were:

1. Projectile stomach (six weeks – eighteen months)
2. Mononucleosis (age two, I thought this was just a teen kissing disease)
3. Asthmatic bronchitis (often)

WE WANT A BABY, GOD!

4. Wearing braces on his feet at night until two years of age. (Both feet turned out at right angles)

5. Three surgeries for a personal problem; age two, four, and ten.

6. Surgery to clip his tongue at the same time of his other surgery. His tongue was so severely tied that the doctor asked me if he could talk. I said, "Yes." I thought he talked very well for a two-year-old, but after the surgery, he talked perfectly!

Todd's physical problems were becoming more and more obvious. He took his first steps at eighteen months. When he did begin walking well and running, he could not stop himself and consequently bounced off walls and furniture or anything in his path. Many times, he carried a big "goose egg" on his head. When friends came over to visit us and Todd would come barreling through the house and bounce off something, they would jump and gasp! It had become so common place; we hardly noticed any more. I'd just say, "Oh it's okay, he does that all the time."

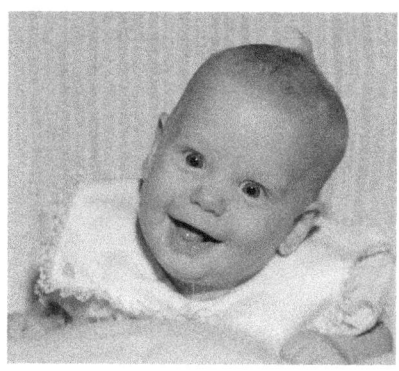

Miraculously My Own

Guess what! Around Todd's third birthday, my husband and I discovered Larry and I were going to have a baby. The following March 16th, God blessed us with a little baby girl, who we named Jill Elaine (Elaine after my sister). Though we had thought about adopting a girl soon, we didn't even think to pray for her! She was a gift, imagine that! We let Todd hold her, and he seemed in awe of his tiny little baby sister.

One morning, I was sitting on the floor of Todd's room next to his chest of drawers. I asked my four-year-old son to hand me his pajamas so I could put them away. They were lying at his feet. He did not respond. I asked him again, still no response. I asked him the third time, my voice now a little louder. I looked up and saw Todd's face as he said, "I---am-m-m." I saw a very confused and fearful little boy. I knew at that moment we had a child with a very serious problem. According to the Department of Health and Human Services, there are one in five children with some kind of mental and/or emotional disorder. Some like Todd with no outward distinctions. Todd was eventually diagnosed with an intermittent short circuit from brain to body, and later in life with bi-polar and obsessive-compulsive disorder.

When Jill was two months old, we were going out to dinner for the first time since she was born. Todd opened the door, lost his balance, and fell smack on his face, which knocked his two front teeth almost out. I grabbed him and shoved his teeth back in place and rushed him to the dentist. One tooth came out then, the other fell out almost a year later.

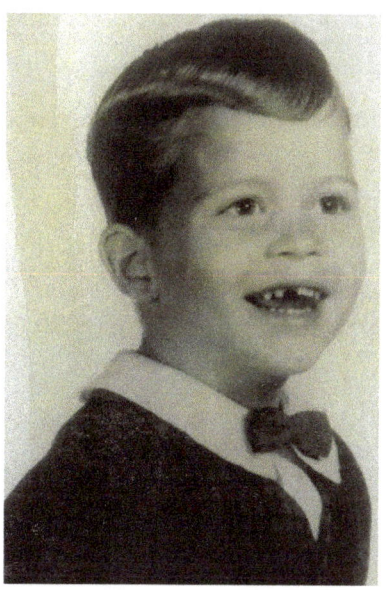

Todd had stopped bouncing off walls now but was still unable to catch himself when he fell. The pediatrician had Todd tested for cerebral palsy because he toe-walked. The test did not show anything because his condition was so minor. The doctor said he was just on the borderline. Todd did eventually stop toe-walking.

Todd was so intelligent, the pediatrician wanted him to start kindergarten, though he was only four years of age. His birthday, October 9th, made him barely old enough to start to school. I was very concerned knowing someone could accidentally push him down and he could be injured, possibly seriously. I expressed my concern to the doctor, and he said, "Todd is so intelligent, he is really ready to go to school." However, he said he would have Todd tested by a psychologist friend who tested children in her home so children were not aware they are being tested. She would test him for both physical and mental abilities. After the physiologist finished testing Todd, she came in and said to us, shaking her head, "No wonder Todd is having so many problems, his intelligence range is as high as ten-year old's." An example of a question I asked him was, "How are paper and coal alike?"

Todd answered, "Well, they both burn." [I was thinking, how are they alike?] However, his physical ability is as young as a one-and-a-half-year-old, and his actual age was four. It was everyone's consensus Todd wait until the next year to attend school.

Todd was five and Jill two when God surprised us with another baby. This time on April 22nd, we had a boy.

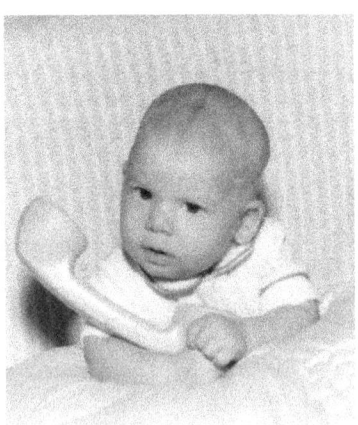

Thank God this pregnancy was uneventful, except I had to have another C-section as my doctor would not let her patients have a normal birth when they had gone through a C-section before. I guess it was a good thing too, because she said my uterus was too thin to carry any more children. If I had carried another baby, it could have killed me and the baby. So, I was glad she insisted I have a C-section again.

Trent was energetic and comical and a tease from the time he could walk and talk. Trent kept me laughing almost continually.

One time, when he had just learned to dress himself, I told him to go get dressed, that we had to go to the store. So, in a little bit, he came out and said, "I ready to go Momma." I turned around and looked at him, and he had his pants on his head and his shirt on like pants, holding my purse and wearing my boots.

***

Important Information to consider before anyone adopts.

I thought when we adopted Todd, especially since he was a newborn, I would just raise him, and he would be like one naturally birthed. This was true as far as the love went. We couldn't have loved Todd more had he been born to us. Having said that, there are many things adoptive parents need to know that I wish we had known. It is so important to gather all information possible. Information is easier to obtain now than it used to be.

    A. Be informed about the birth mother, father, and also the grandparents: (paternal and maternal).

    1) To know their ages, health, family history, and any addictions.

    2) To know the family's education and careers will help foresee the child's future potential and motivation.

    B. If the child is not from the same culture:

    1) Learn all you can about his/her culture.

    2) Be informed as to the religious background.

Especially if adopted child is not a baby.

    It is also wise to search for possible generational curses "visited" (passed down) on any child adopted or not. It could be physical, mental, or spiritual problems, or a combination of two or all three.

    Teaching about generational curses is especially needed when you adopt, because only through God's Word can you fight some of the unimaginable baggage you may be adopting along with your child. God has promised in Deut. 7: 9 (NASB) loving kindness to the *thousandth generations*, to the people who love Him and keep His commandments. God is not referring just to the Ten Commandments, though they would certainly be included.

WE WANT A BABY, GOD!

We are heirs to the blessings of Abraham that God promised the Israelites; if we keep His laws, He will keep His covenant of love with us. See Deut. 7: 12 – 14, NASB. One of those promises is from Deut. 7: 13 (NASB), that *He will bless the fruit of the womb...* blessings always follow our obedience, but we must know His commandments in order to obey them. We are under the covenant of grace (unmerited favor) now, but blessing will be received through obedience.

However, to those who worship anything other than the Lord our God (idols), God says in Exodus 20:5-6 (NASB), *"I am a jealous God, visiting the iniquity of the fathers on the children, on the third and fourth generations of those who hate me."*

I know what you are thinking because I know what I would have thought if someone had given me this information when we adopted Todd. I would have said, "Well, that is just borrowing trouble!" However, God is actually preparing us through His Word. He says in II Tim. 3:16 (HCSB) that, God's Word is *"profitable for: [1] Teaching, [2] Rebuking, [3] Correcting, and, [4] Training in righteousness, so that the man of God may be complete, equipped for every good work."* (Numbering Mine)

Adoption is certainly a *good work*, and it is very important to be equipped to handle the tremendous responsibility of raising any child, especially one who has special needs. After adoption and being informed of the baby's biological family health, physical and mental, it is important to:

1) Dedicate the baby to God (have the pastor bless the child; and to encourage the church family to help in anyway needed).
2) Be faithful to God (Church attendance, etc.).
3) Have daily devotional with the child (family time).
4) Have one on one time.

It is very hard to be a single parent and raise any child, but if a child has special needs, it is next to impossible without someone to come along side and be a stable support. Sometimes even a spouse is not that support. Some people just do not know how to be a support, or they just may not want to be supportive. If a spouse does not believe in God, it would be hard for them to believe God will help. A single parent needs to find a live-in sibling, aunt, uncle, or even a faithful friend to rely on as a supporter and will provide back-up when a child is out of control. The church family is also a great means of support. Some may even be fill-in caretakers when the family needs a break.

Our biggest setback when we learn what God says to do is not do it. When we read the Word and it gives us the solution and the promise if we obey, the promise sounds just too wonderful to be true. In Mark 11: 24 (HCSB), Jesus says, *"Therefore, I tell you all the things you pray and ask for, believe that you have received them, and you shall have them."* That is an awesome promise and so difficult to believe that we try every way we can to prove it couldn't mean what it says, or that it could apply to us or our situation. Of course, what we pray for has to be in line with God's Word and reflect His nature and character.

We need to read God's Word as if He is speaking directly to us because He is. His word is alive, and it all applies to us. See, Matt. 5:17 it tells us that all Scripture (law and prophets) applies today except those that Jesus came to fulfill, which He did and proclaimed on the cross, *"It is finished"* John 19:30, (NASB).

I started putting my name in place of the person God was talking to whenever it applied to life and godliness. The Bible came alive in my heart, and I had a burning desire to read and learn more of what He was saying to me.

God was so pleased when we brought a child into our home that would not have had a godly family in which to grow up. God calls that in, James 1:27 (KJV), *"pure religion."*

Once informed of in all areas of the child's background, it is so vital that we understand and be in tune with the Holy Spirit. He is the most important "Helper" of all.

Miraculously My Own

Our most gracious heavenly Father,
Help us to look to you, and your Spirit
to guide us, for the answers as to
where, when, and how,
we should make our decisions.

In Jesus name,
Amen.

Chapter 3

Happy "Daze"

Consider it pure joy my brother, whenever you face trials of many kinds Because you know that the testing of your faith develops perseverance.

— James 1:2-3, NIV

Todd was a very happy, intelligent little boy. He loved school. In kindergarten, Open House Night, I discovered Todd had an artistic talent. He had painted with poster paint a large Easter bunny holding an Easter basket and different color eggs raining down. When I went over to the painting, I saw it said "Todd Lacey" on the bottom. I asked the teacher, "Did Todd paint that?"

She said, "Yes, isn't that marvelous?"

I said, "He has never even drawn a circle at home!"

As I was admiring the painting, Todd said, "Mommy, see it's raining eggs." The picture had all pastel-colored eggs; yellow, lavender, and white coming down from the sky. I thought that was such a creative idea for a little kindergartner. It was so cute, and I liked it so much that I had it framed to hang on our wall at home.

Miraculously My Own

 I discovered Todd had to be inspired to draw or paint. It was in the second grade when he had another inspiration. He drew a race car with a silhouette of a man inside. The teacher was so impressed that he put it up on the wall.

 The next inspiration was while we were visiting my sister Elaine in Baton Rouge, LA. The astronauts had landed on the moon. When they returned home, Todd was so excited he drew the capsule coming down by parachutes and landing in the ocean.

 My sister was so amazed at his drawing ability that she took us to see *Buckskin Bill*, a children's T.V. program, and Buckskin Bill showed Todd's pictures on T.V.

 Though Todd was excited to have them shown on T.V., to my knowledge he has never drawn anything else.

Happy "Daze"

When I realized he wasn't interested in drawing anymore, I thought about his fascination with bugs and insects or anything that crept or crawled. I heard that Cal State Fullerton was offering a children's class on bugs and insects, so I signed Todd up. He was very excited until we got to the first class and they were mounting butterflies. They had to put them alive in a jar of ether, and when they died, they pinned them to a board. Todd was upset by this and wanted no part of it. I told him they would do different things with and about bugs, but he would not go back to class.

We also discovered Todd was musically inclined. Todd liked to watch Lawrence Welk. He especially liked Myron Floran, who played the accordion. He also liked Anita Aris, who played the violin. When he was very young, (about three or four) and he would hear Anita start to play her violin, even if he was in another room, he would run in and sit down in front of the T.V to watch until she finished playing.

One day, the highly acclaimed Milton Mann Studios came to our house and asked if we had any children who might be interested in learning to play the accordion. We talked to Todd and he said yes, he would like to play an accordion.

Miraculously My Own

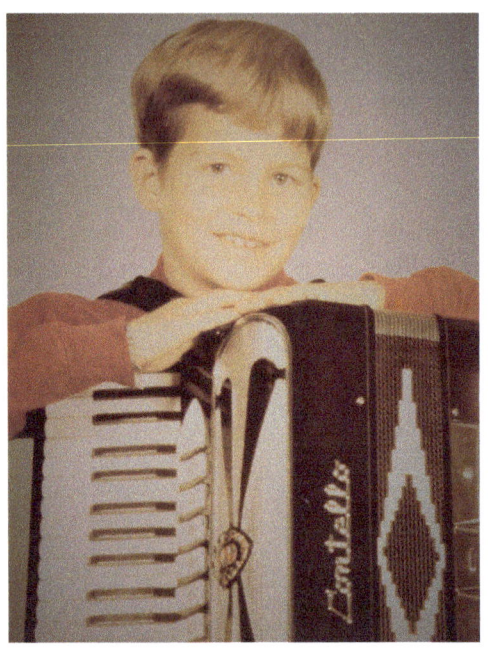

    Todd loved playing the accordion. He had a wonderful teacher who did an excellent job, and Todd was always ready to play a solo at his recitals. He did remarkably well. I was amazed especially given his slow coordination, that he was able to manage playing the accordion so skillfully. For the first time, Todd was able to do something some of his friends couldn't do. He was gaining so much confidence, we were thinking just maybe all our concerns were behind us.

    When Todd was ten, we moved from Fullerton to Yucaipa. We were so happy we could enroll him in the Milton Mann Studios in San Bernardino. However, this experience destroyed all the confidence Todd had gained. The environment was so different than it had been in Fullerton. The teacher smoked and allowed parents to smoke

Happy "Daze"

in the class area. Todd had private lessons in a tiny room, and the teacher smoked the whole time he was teaching him. Todd seemed uncomfortable with the smoke, but never complained as he accepted what adults did as their right.

The reason Todd was getting private lessons was because he was the only kid in that class level, which would have made him ready for band three. There was no band three, so the teacher decided to put Todd in band four. When the teacher passed out music to the class, Todd had no idea how to play it. I told the teacher to keep him in band two, that he was not ready to jump into level four yet. But he said, "It's ok; I know what Todd can do. I don't expect him to be able to do all the band four music." Unfortunately, Todd did not understand when the teacher yelled at the class and said, "If you kids don't start practicing your music and preparing a solo each week, I'm going to start taking away stars," that the teacher didn't mean him. Todd was so proud of all his stars, and I was sure the other kids were too. I was very upset, and I said to the teacher, "How can you take away the stars the kids have already earned?" He said he wasn't talking about Todd. That Todd always had a solo prepared. He missed my point. Todd became so frustrated that he could not do the music that band four was doing, and he stopped all practicing.

It totally deflated him. I was so desperate because he had finally found something he could do well and was also very good for his coordination and self-confidence, that I tried to force him to practice. When I was at the point of standing over him with a belt, I realized it was over. I was hurt for Todd and angry at his instructor.

His old instructor from Fullerton, a marvelously skillful man, excellent with children inspiring them to always do their best, heard I had pulled Todd out of the class. He called me and said, "Oh, please don't take Todd out of his accordion class." I told him I had to, as Todd would no longer touch his accordion as a result of what that instructor had done. This was an unfortunate incident because the Milton Mann organization helps so many young children develop their musical talents.

Things went downhill from then on. Todd's confidence was destroyed. He no longer wanted to work on much of anything. This was his pattern when he became overwhelmed.

He did eventually join the swim team, but he was already turning fifteen and it was very hard to be on a team starting at that age. He usually came in last. He did get some winning ribbons because there weren't many in his age group. However, the next year he would not sign up because he said he was tired of coming in last. I was sorry he quit because he looked great and was probably the healthiest, he had ever been or would be.

Happy "Daze"

It broke my heart when I saw this picture. It shows how he had become discouraged with everything going on in his life.

Miraculously My Own

Dear father in heaven
Thank you for caring for our family.
Teach us patience. In Jesus name,
Amen.

Chapter 4

THE TEEN YEARS

"When pride comes then comes dishonor, but with the humble is wisdom"

— Prov. 11:2, NASB

When Todd was quite young, his pediatrician predicted that he would likely be mentally and physically "normal" around age twenty-five. Then he added, "That is, if he doesn't get so emotionally messed up during his teen years."

Most every parent will have a difficult time dealing with their teenagers. However, parents of children with physical and/or emotional problems will experience heavier burdens and have extra troublesome battles to fight. Every teen has a need to be accepted, especially by their peers. At school, teens contrive all kinds of rules and regulations for acceptance in their particular clique.

During junior high and high school, some kids are rejected by certain *in* groups, so those rejected have a tendency to form their own group. Rebelling, they act as if they *"don't care"* and can become troublemakers. Some get into drugs, some have sexual problems, others have trouble with the law, and some have all of the above.

During Todd's teen years, problems began to manifest

such as angry outbursts for no particular reason. Rebelling when we needed him to promptly get ready to go to school, church, and anywhere that time was of an essence. Every morning before school, our home was in turmoil as we fought to get Todd out the door in time for school. Physical fighting would occur when we would try to force his co-operation.

Todd would not help-out around the house; he would just lie around and listen to heavy metal music. Since drugs were prevalent, he eventually began doing some drugs.

What a blessing and we are so grateful that Todd never became addicted to drugs. I'm sure he thought, *I'll do anything if only kids will accept me.* Todd never verbalized that, but I believe that was how he felt. I wanted so much to stop the hurt and rejection.

Over the years, kids teased Todd unmercifully. Once in junior high, they stood in a circle around him, gave him a fly, dared him to eat it, and then called him, "fly eater." Once on the bus, the kids took Todd's watch off. However, the boy that took it home had a good mother; she called me up and made her son apologize and give the watch back.

The principal of the junior high told us we had to put Todd in Wildwood School. It was a school for kids who didn't "fit in," and for kids who had been in trouble with the law and lived at the boy's home in town.

He also told us they were afraid Todd might hurt himself on a dare, like jump off a building. That was another reason they felt he needed to go to the other school. We were certain Todd would never do such a thing, but we agreed thinking he *would* have more one-on-one teaching time.

What a disaster that school proved to be for Todd. Allowing him to associate with other troubled teens certainly was one of the biggest mistakes we could have made. The Bible warns us, *"Do not be deceived: bad company corrupts good morals"* I Corinthians 1:33, (NASB). The kids would persuade Todd to do all kinds of things, like letting the air out of the principal's car tires. Once, knowing Todd's slow reaction, they bet him they could break a pencil before he could, then they charged him for losing the bet. I know I sound like I'm saying Todd had no responsibility for his actions, but because of his need to have friends, he was easy to manipulate. We were continually trying to make him responsible. Without the help of God, we were fighting a losing battle.

One day, I happened to pick up the phone when Todd was talking to a kid from the boy's home, and I heard the kid threaten him. He said, "You get the money for the bet or I'll cut your throat."

When I asked Todd why he let that kid talk to him like that, he said, "Oh he was just kidding." Then on a Sunday (soon after the phone call), some kids drove up to our house, and Todd went outside to talk to them. I could tell it was not a friendly visit.

When they left, we asked Todd what they wanted. He

finally told us he had to have eighteen dollars to pay off a bet. He told them he didn't have the money, and they said, "Well, rip off your parents." Larry and I were so upset with Todd and those kids that Larry immediately took Todd, went to each kid's home, and talked to the parents. Larry found that to be quite an eye-opening experience. He said the parents were indifferent and unconcerned. Larry paid Todd's bet off and told Todd, the other kids, and their parents no more betting had better go on in the future.

Things continued to get worse, so we took Todd out of Wildwood School and got him a private tutor. But hiring a tutor was not the answer either. Todd was a very social person and really needed social interaction. He became increasingly more frustrated.

One day when he was fourteen, I told Todd to dust his room, and when he didn't do it, I started dusting it myself. He became enraged with me. He said, "I was going to do it," and he just flipped out. He smashed pictures on the walls, turned over chests and beds, destroyed most everything he could in the house, and then ran outside. I ran down our hill to the house of some friends. By God's grace, the husband who worked at a juvenile camp was home. He was able to calm Todd down enough for us to take him to the psychologist who Todd had seen from fifth through eighth grade, and she was now a psychiatrist. We think she unintentionally drove a wedge between us and our son.

When we took Todd to see her, she wanted us to take

him to a hospital in La Habra for evaluation and treatment. She made the comment to Todd, "When you get to the hospital, Todd, *they* will be on your side!"

I said, "Well, we are all on Todd's side!"

That remark made me think back to a particular incident when Todd was seeing her on a regular basis. She had given Todd a heavy metal tape. He had told her, "My parents don't like for me to listen to that kind of music." She had said to him, "Well, that's okay, I'll talk to them."

We had never said Todd could not listen to that kind of music, but we didn't like it and we had insisted he not play it loud. We believed the psychologist had put us in a precarious position with Todd by saying she would talk to us. If we had said, "No, he cannot have the tape," she would have been siding against us. If we had said, "Yes," then she would have become the authority over our family values. We had ended up agreeing, but to "save face," we had added we still had the same rule, *not to play it loud!* There were other incidents, but that was one example of why we felt she complicated our relationship with our son.

This taught us a very important lesson. We needed to choose a Christian psychologist who was recommended by a Christian friend or pastor. We had not done that. We didn't realize the importance of Christian counseling. A child must have a psychologist that will give children and their parents scriptures to feed on. Their own ideas from their educational training or even their years of experience are not enough.

GOD DEALS WITH OUR PRIDE

Pride goes before destruction and a haughty spirit before a fall.

— Proverbs 16: 18, NIV

Todd was admitted to the hospital in La Habra for tests and treatment, after the rampage. I could almost write another book on his hospital experience. Todd was kept drugged most of the time. He was so drugged that he fell off the pew at church. It was our routine to pick him up at the hospital on Sundays, take him to church, and then out to lunch. We sometimes got a hotel, hoping he would go swimming or something, but all he could do was sleep.

When we complained to the hospital staff, they gave him "uppers" before we came to pick him up so he could stay awake.

Though that hospital came highly recommended, we were appalled at what went on there. Nurses would sit in their stations and smoke with a sign posted "No Smoking" right in the station window. I thought, *What a conflicting example for teens in mental and emotional distress.*

One night, Todd and one of the other boys snuck out of

the hospital. Todd called us from a restaurant in Riverside and said they had walked all the way from the hospital. Distraught and frightened for them, Larry and I went to pick them up. We took the boys back to the hospital, letting the staff know how we felt about their security and medical treatment.

Because we were so embarrassed, we wanted to stop all the turmoil *before everyone knew* what was going on in our family. God exposed our *pride* by allowing people to know about Todd. God told us that secret things belong to Him.

We could no longer keep our family secrets. We began to change our prideful thinking. I no longer cared that my house was in shambles, what people thought about me or my family, or why we weren't doing certain things at church, having people over to our home like we used to, and whatever else we weren't doing that people thought we should be doing. I realized God was doing a work in all of us. I just wanted our family and my son to be well and happy again.

The day before Todd was released from the hospital, they recommended a place for us to have Todd committed. I cried almost all the way home. I was by myself and weeping so much I could hardly see the road.

I prayed, *"Father, you did not give me this child to lock him up for the rest of his life! I will trust you to help us do the right thing for him and for us."* God gave me peace, and I calmed down as I drove the rest of the way home.

Pride said, "*Our* child will not take drugs!" That would have been a good confession if we had said it in faith toward God. But no! We meant *we* would see to it, one way or the other. We also tried to stop Todd's O.C.D. (obsessive compulsive, disorder) mannerisms like coughing at us, pumping the handles on the water faucets, taking an hour and longer showers. So, we began a barrage of punishments ranging from restrictions to whippings to out-and-out, knock-down, drag-outs.

As Todd got older, he became more and more difficult to live with. He would defy my husband and me and put up a fight about most anything. In order to stop the fighting and before someone got injured or worse, I would tell Jill or Trent to call the police. It was usually between Todd and his father to get them to stop fighting.

We prayed, not knowing how to pray in faith, made contracts, and gave ultimatums. Nothing worked. A child like Todd needs supernatural guidance, but we were not listening to the counsel of the Holy Spirit at that time.

All children benefit when God is involved of course; however, some are more vulnerable, and Satan takes advantage of them and will, "kill, steal, or destroy" them in whatever way he can (John 10:10, NASB). All we have to do is look at schools like Columbine to see that!

We were beginning to experience the truth of God's Word, *"Pride goes before destruction"* (Proverbs 16:18, NIV). Our home was in shambles. Todd was an emotional

THE TEEN YEARS

mess; the rest of us weren't much better. Todd thought he hated us, and we were beginning to wonder if we hated him. When thoughts of *hate* entered my mind, I would hear my mother's words ring in my ears, "*Oh, no, Joyce, you don't hate anyone. Everyone has a soul. You just hate what they do.*" It was still good to hear her sound advice. My mom died when I was twenty-eight. Although I didn't have my parents very long, they were truly blessings, and they made a profound impact on my life.

I continued to ask God for wisdom to help Todd and our family get back on track (see Prov. 3:13 -180). This was a difficult time for the whole family. Jill (eleven) and Trent (nine) loved Todd, but they were fighting their own battles with embarrassment and anger. Even though they understood why so much attention was focused on Todd, it was still very unsettling for them.

Soon after Todd was released from the hospital, we brought him home, and he ran away. He ended up at a lady's home who gave him dinner and offered to take him home. He had her driving all over Yucaipa, not because he didn't know where he lived, but because he didn't want to come home. She finally dropped him off at the sheriff's station, where he called us to come get him. He said that the lady talked to him about, "the prodigal son." Obviously, this precious lady was sent by God.

These difficult times helped me become confident in God. I learned I could trust Him completely, and therefore I no longer worried. God *will* take care of our children when we leave them in His hands.

Things continued to be very difficult for Todd after returning to high school from the hospital. A kid pulled his shirt off and flushed it down the toilet. When I picked him up after school, kids would taunt him, shouting lies so I could hear, things like he was smoking, doing drugs at school, and that he cussed the teacher out, but the teachers told me Todd was always polite to them. When Todd got home, he would walk right through the house to his room, slam the door, and not come out. He would turn on the heavy metal music.

I found out later some of the lyrics were really harmful, telling kids that life wasn't worth living, their parents didn't understand them, to do their own thing, and they didn't have to listen to anyone in authority. Todd saturated himself with that negative music.

Todd himself never complained or told us anything that kids did to him, other kids, teachers, and friends would come to us and tell us. Those were the times we should have talked to Todd and prayed with him. We never knew what to do when we heard of the things that happened to him, so we just ignored the incidents, hoping they would either go away or that Todd would eventually learn to deal with them. But we needed God!

After Todd dropped out of school, he did the most drastic thing I could have imagined that he would do. At

THE TEEN YEARS

age seventeen, he took off with a cult. This cult was called "The Lightning Amen." Most people called them the "White Sheets" because they walked around in white sheets and bare feet. They didn't believe in killing animals, and since most shoes are made of leather, they went barefooted. So, Todd threw his brand-new shoes away and went with them to Texas. However, they dropped him off at Victory Outreach, a Christian Rehabilitation Center in Texas, several days later. He said the White Sheets told him they were tired of waiting for him all the time.

Todd said they were very good to him at Victory Outreach, but he and another boy decided to leave and hop a train. The other kid made it on to the train, but Todd did not. Todd decided to hitch a ride home. A truck driver stopped to pick him up and bought him something to eat and gave him $4.00. He continued to hitch-hike home. A young man stopped to pick him up. This young man said that he never picked up hitch hikers, but God told him to stop and pick him up. This *God sent* young man brought Todd all the way home to Yucaipa, playing Christian music the whole time. Todd called home when he got to Yucaipa to ask us if he *could* come home. We said, "Of course," and offered to pick him up, but the young man said he would bring him home. I wanted to thank that young man, but he just dropped Todd off and left.

God took care of Todd so many times. It is so encouraging to know that God loves our children even more than we do.

Time and again, when Todd would get angry and take off, the Holy Spirit would direct me right to where he was. All these situations taught Larry and me enough humility to begin truly seeking God to listen to the Holy Spirit in order to learn what to do.

I especially wanted Todd to realize his worth as a person. He was so despondent and angry and guilt-ridden, he often talked of suicide. I knew he would have to be convinced of God's love and our love. Showing our love at this time was a tall order because almost every word came out in anger when we spoke to him.

Praise the Lord, God was faithful. He continued to teach us to love Todd unconditionally and recognize we were in a spiritual battle. Through each trial, God dealt with our pride. As the title scripture in this chapter says, "When pride comes, then comes dishonor, but with the humble is wisdom" (Proverbs 11:2, NASB).

God's desire is for us to pass on what we learned to others, and I want to help parents by telling our story. Hopefully, they will avoid some of the pitfalls we encountered. God and His Word are wonderful. When we learn what He says, and we do it, the truth of His Word becomes evident and teaches us how to receive the promised abundant life.

THE TEEN YEARS

Father God,
You were able to strip us of a lot of our pride.
We are humbled and ready to listen to your wise council.

Thank You.

In Jesus name,
Amen.

Chapter 5

Unconditional Love

"But now abide faith, hope love, these three; but the greatest of these is LOVE"

— I Cor. 13:13, NASB

God's *agape* or unconditional love is the key to *all* successful relationships. Romans 5:8 (NIV) says, "God demonstrates His own love toward us in this: While we were yet sinners, Christ died for us."

Our unconditional love was really tested during Todd's teen years. There was so much turmoil going in our home. I needed to understand why uncontrolled anger was so prevalent. I have since learned that the emotions behind anger are 1) *hurt,* 2) *fear,* and/or 3) *frustration.* At one time or the other, I felt each of those emotions.

I felt *hurt* because I believed Todd thought his problems were because he was adopted. He said to me one day, "Don't kiss me because I have different germs than you do because I am adopted."

I chuckled and said, "You don't have different germs than we do, you have different genes." That just made me think he was trying to figure out why he was having so many problems and thought it must be because he was adopted.

We wanted Todd to know how excited and happy we were to have adopted him, how precious he was to us, and how much we wanted him to be happy. However, I suppose we thought he would receive this knowledge by osmosis, as I don't recall ever sitting him down and telling him those things. We said we loved him, but specific words telling him how precious he was were never said.

It would have been more important to have expressed the feelings of excitement and fulfillment he brought into our lives more than anything we could ever do monetarily or physically for him. Every child deserves this validation. However, adopted and special needs children require confirmation of their worth even more.

It was my *fear* that he would not ever be happy or have a productive life.

I read in God's Word, (I John 4:18, NASB), *"...Perfect love casts out fear."* I wanted to know that kind of love. As I got to know God more intimately, He helped me to learn more about giving and receiving *agape* love.

Fear is Satan's playground. He was able to ravage Job through fear. In Job 3:25 (NIV), Job said, *"What I feared has come upon me, what I dreaded has happened to me."* God works and protects through our faith. Satan works and destroys through fear, as he did in Job's case.

From the time Todd was small, we tried to motivate him in many ways: physical therapy, psycho-therapy, accordion lessons for a while, guitar lesions, even a special children's class on insects. It was *frustrating* to see so little fruit come from our efforts.

Hurt, fear, and frustration blocked our ability to receive from God. Anger and the subsequent emotions opened the door for Satan to work because they were in direct opposition to faith. Hebrews 11: 6 (NIV) says, *"Without faith it is impossible to please God."* The Amplified Bible tells us in Gal. 5:6 that faith is activated, energized, expressed, and worked through love.

Eph.4:26-27 (AMP) says, *"When angry do not sin; do not ever let your wrath (your exasperation, your fury or indignation) last until the sun goes down. Leave no such room or foothold for the devil [give no opportunity to him]."*

Todd developed obsessive compulsive disorder (O.C.D.). I just could not accept or tolerate his looking at the bottom of his shoe, turning lights on and off, pumping the water faucets, smelling his fork before he eats, looking under his plate, and taking hour long and more showers.

My prideful attitude toward O.C.D. caused many outbursts and confrontations with Todd because I would try to correct him or stop him. Over time, with researching mental disorders and beginning to understand the power of prayer, I finally realized I had to *accept and learn* about Todd's emotional problems.

Larry and I did not realize that God could remove generational curses that were *"visited"* (handed down) from Todd's biological family. I don't know if O.C.D. is inherited or not, but tendencies toward mental disorders definitely are.

God removes family curses *if* we are obedient to the conditions stated in many scriptures, which are to keep His commandments and not to worship idols (see Num., 14: 18-20, Deut. 5:8-10, Exodus, 20: 4-6, Exodus, 34: 6-7).

Idols refer not only to statues of wood or stone made by man, but anything that we would put before God. They would be things that interfere with our personal time with God like money, pleasure, or even church work or church functions, anything that would pull us away from a personal time with God. The Bible says:

> *The Lord, the Lord, the compassionate and gracious God, slow to anger, abounding in love and faithfulness, maintaining love to thousands, and forgiving wickedness, rebellion and sin, yet He does not leave the guilty unpunished; He punishes the children and their children for the sin of the fathers to the third and fourth generations.*
>
> — Exodus 34:6-7, NIV

Had we have known, and assuming we had met the conditions in regards to idol worship, we would have needed to really search our hearts as to what and where we were devoting our time. When we adopted Todd, we didn't have him dedicated. It was not a common practice at the church we attended. We could have asked the pastor to

Unconditional Love

pray against generational curses, though I have never seen that done at a dedication. Larry and I also needed to pray against generational curses, rebuking them in the name of Jesus.

Todd would have been free of any family curses that had been handed down to him from his biological family. Studying the promises of God and how they are received is a very important study. We learned that God's *love* is always *unconditional*, but His promises are all *conditional*. When searching God's Word, we find every promise in the Bible carries with it a condition; even our salvation (though we are saved by grace) requires that we receive Jesus as the way, the truth, and the life.

John 14:6 (NIV) tells us what Jesus says (the condition) is in order to have access to the Father: *"No one comes to the Father except through Me."* Some of us were taught that we had to earn God's love and salvation, but He says,

> *Because of His great love for us, God who is rich in mercy, made us alive with Christ even when we were dead in transgressions…, For it is by grace you have been saved, through faith – and this is not from yourselves, it is the gift of God – not by works, so that no one can boast.*
>
> — Ephesians, 2: 4-5, 8- 9, NIV

The first and foremost condition in learning to love unconditionally and resisting family curses is to know God and accept Jesus as our Lord and personal Savior, because that is how we become part of the family of God.

When we are born again, we are new creatures in Christ Jesus.

II Cor. 5: 17 (KJV) says, *"Old things are passed away; all things become new!"*

When we go to the doctor and we have to give our family history, there may be a history of heart disease or cancer or mental illness. Isaiah 53:4-5 and I Peter 2:24 tells us that Jesus bore our sins, griefs, sicknesses, and carried our diseases so we now have a new family history.

I'm the first to confess that it is very hard to have faith without any doubt, but it is my goal. When I have obeyed conditions specified in a promise, God has always proved faithful to that promise. It is good to see God fulfilling promises in my life, as I trust Him completely. I know what the Word says, and I believe it intellectually, but deep in my heart many times I have had doubts that God will answer *"Yes"* to my prayer.

Larry and I are excited about developing faith that can move mountains. See Mark 11:23 and Heb. 12:2 (KJV) that says that Jesus is the *"Author and finisher of our faith."*

He helps us develop our faith by exercising *agape* love. Gal. 5:6 (NASB) says what *matters faith is working through Love.* Many times, I have heard Christians say, "God always answers prayers, but He sometimes says *yes* and sometimes, *no?"* That is not biblical. We have to know

God's will in a matter *before* we pray. How do we do that? His Word is His will. (See Romans 12:2.) When we know what His Word says in regards to our need we can pray in faith without any doubt. We can pray, knowing God will answer, *"Yes"* to our prayer!

> *But as God is faithful, our word to you is not **"yes"** and "no." For the Son of God, Christ Jesus, Who was preached among you by us... was not yes and no, but yes in Him. For as many as may be the promises of God, in Him they are YES; wherefore, also by Him is our Amen to the glory of God through us.*
>
> — II Cor. 1: 18-20, NASB

Though some of Todd's problems were genetic, some were due possibly to an unhealthy pregnancy. If we had known how to pray and what to pray for, and how to believe what we were praying for, God would have said, "Yes," and healed Todd, spirit, soul, and body!

How do we know? We know because of God's Word, His promises, and the examples of believing prayer. At this writing, Todd is forty-nine years old. Is it too late for him? No, however, faith and the condition to receive the promises are his responsibility too now. We can agree (prayer of agreement) and stand with him, but Todd now must believe God can and will heal him.

We keep hope alive. God will always do what we

ask in faith and when we are obedient to the conditions recorded in His Word. It is my prayer that you believe and know without a doubt that God wants to heal your child. There may be a trial period to test your faith, as God tested Abraham and Sarah; God uses times of trial to equip us and to develop our faith.

Unconditional love is a choice, not a feeling. It is also a command from God that we love Him and one another. When I learned these principles from the study of the Scripture and personal time with God, I made the decision to love Todd unconditionally.

I started by taking him out to lunch when I picked him up from high school. There was no bus, and he was not able to drive because his mind and body would not always work together. I began saying every day, "I love you, Todd." It was hard for me to say because I still felt angry. Todd did not respond at first, but as God opened my eyes to how difficult life was for Todd, I began to feel compassion and love for him again. After a few weeks of telling him I loved him, he said, "I love you too, Mom." How wonderful that sounded. I really felt a breakthrough, although many tough years would lay ahead.

Todd had just got out of the hospital in La Habra, and he was having a hard time adjusting to high school. His teen years were so difficult he ended up having to spend time in jail. Our hearts were broken. We wanted to do something to encourage him, so each of us wrote a prayer letter to comfort and encourage him as best we could. (You will read those prayers in the prayer chapter of this book.)

Todd wasn't the only one having a difficult time. It would have been good to have given each of our children more one on one time and to have been aware of their individual struggles and needs. We were so caught up in all the problems dealing with Todd, we were not aware Jill and Trent were suffering from the backlash of family turmoil.

We did not think that a good performance was most deserving of our love and reward, but that was the impression our children picked up from us. So, when our children thought they are not accomplishing what was expected of them, it was very hard for them to feel unconditionally loved.

Some children think they have to prove themselves worthy of love by pushing themselves to perform. They may even go looking for love in all the wrong places and receive only a deceptive or destructive kind of affection perceived as love. In their hearts, they believe they can never live up to their own or others' expectations and therefore never feel deserving of unconditional love.

I understand psychologists now say some young girls become high achievers because of their need to be validated as a person of worth, that this can also be a root cause of anorexia and/or bulimia. Some children get into drugs as Todd did. Jill thought she had to make straight A's in school and always had to win in sports or games.

Trent became the class clown.

Larry and I needed to make more of an effort to give Todd, Jill, and Trent individual attention, doing something with them that they really liked to do. We showed them how much we enjoyed just being with them and complimented them often, looking for the positive things about each of them and then telling them.

I hear you say, "What if there are no positive things?" I can really understand that statement. There were times when my children were in their teens that complimenting them seemed impossible. However, giving each one special time will win their respect and positive response. With God's help, all things are possible.

One on one time needs to start when they are very young. But if time has gotten away from you, as it did for Larry and me, I will encourage you by saying it is never too late to begin to build up their self-esteem.

Jill and Trent were grown when we became aware of the struggles they were having. We asked God to help us regain those lost years with them and with Todd too.

Praise God; He did redeem our time when we asked Him. We now have developed a good relationship with all our children. We continue to work on our relationships with each of them, knowing how important it is to keep communication open between us. When we love one another, God is pleased, we glorify Him, and we all benefit. God's Word says in Eph. 4:29 (NASB), *"Let no*

Unconditional Love

unwholesome word proceed from Our mouth, but only such a word as is good for edification according to the need of the of the moment, that it may give grace to those who hear."

Our Great and Mighty God,

You have taught us about (agape) unconditional love, through Your Word and friends who supported us, through good times and bad.

Thank You,
In Jesus name,
Amen

Chapter 6

Forever Friends
(Better Than a "Shrink")

Just as Lotion and Fragrance gives sensual delight,
A sweet friendship refreshes the soul.

— Prov. 27: 9, MSG

One of the great things God has done throughout my life is to provide me with incredible friends. I wish I could mention them all and their helpful contributions.

This may seem an unrelated chapter in a book about my son, Todd. However, it is my desire to show the value and importance of accumulating "forever friends."

Perhaps, over the years, you have had difficulty developing lasting friendships. It is never too late to acquire them. God always has scripture to meditate on that will help us with any situation. A tried and true one is Proverbs 18:24a (NKJV), which says, "A man who has friends must show himself friendly." Maybe you are easily offended, even if a friend is trying to be of help. Here is another great scripture to meditate on if that has been a problem for you: "Faithful are the wounds of a friend" (Prov. 27:6, NASB).

I want to begin my friendship stories when I was three years old. During the depression, my family--Dad, Mom,

Miraculously My Own

and my sister Elaine and I--moved to California from Arkansas. Many of our friends had moved to California, and they all seemed to do well.

I had a half-brother, my mom's son Jessie Willis. His father died with typhoid fever when my mom was eight months pregnant with him. Jessie lived in Gardena, California, and he wanted us to come and stay with his family until we found a place to live, so we did. After a few months we found a duplex in Fullerton, California, right behind Jean (Scratton) Brown. Jean became a forever friend to my sister and also to me.

More about Jean and all she is to us later in this chapter.

While in Arkansas, my family became close friends of the Pennington family. The Penningtons moved to California before we did. When we moved to Fullerton, we were only a few miles from Buena Park where they lived. Their daughter, June, was a couple of years older than my sister; June was like a sister to both of us. My sister, who was my best friend, took me most everywhere she went, including overnight stays at June's house.

Our families worshiped together and sang together at church functions. We were like one big family. Elaine was twelve, June was fourteen, and I was seven. We sang as a trio. June's dad, my dad, Elaine, and June were a quartet. We continued to sing together until Elaine married and moved away when I was fourteen.

June married Jim Pennington (no relation), so she

Forever Friends

became June (Pennington) Pennington! June and her husband Jim became close friends of mine. My sister had moved to Florida. Jim was in the service and had been sent to the Korean conflict, and June moved in with her parents. I would go and spend nights with her and bake fruit cakes etc. to send to Jim. I had a boyfriend in the service at that time as well, so I sent a fruit cake to him.

After my father died, my mom, sister, and I moved to Buena Park. I was in the sixth grade and a little frightened my first day at school. There was one girl who came up to me. Her name was Sandra Sanderson, and she said, "Hi, I'm Sandra, who are you?" We became best friends. Sandra had a horse, and did we ever have fun riding all over Buena Park hills. I loved Sandra and her mom, Pansy. I think my mom and Sandra's mom were cut out of the same mold. They were truly wonderful Christian mothers.

Sandra and I parted ways for a while during high school, not because of any kind of animosity between us; our lives were just going in different directions. We renewed our friendship after each of us married. When Larry and I moved to Yucaipa, Sandra and I didn't keep in touch as often, but I knew she was there for me if or when I might have needed her.

We met Don and Patsy Lindsey when we attended The Church of Christ in Santa Ana, and there we became good friends. Every year, we invited them to join us for Thanksgiving, and I think they always accepted. They liked to say they came to eat my burnt turkey, and that was because I fixed the Thompson Turkey recipe. (Entire recipe is online.) This recipe did make the turkey black because it required a paste of:

12 egg yolks,
2 T Mustard,
6 cloves garlic,
6 T onion juice,
1 T salt
3/4ths tsp. cayenne,
2 T lime juice,
1 cup flour enough for a past,
3 cups cider, and 1 cup water.

This turkey was the juiciest turkey one could make, but it was a big undertaking.

When we moved to Yucaipa, they continued to come and visit, particularly on Thanksgiving. One Thanksgiving in Yucaipa, it actually snowed. So, we all made snow ice cream. Our kids, Todd, Jill, and Trent, and their girls Nancy and Susan, played in the snow and had a great time. One thing the kids liked to do was to put on a play to entertain us. We loved their ingenuity and talent, and we thoroughly enjoyed watching them.

At this writing, my sister went to be with the Lord in August 2004, losing her battle with breast cancer, and June

Forever Friends

joined her six months later after her battle with lung cancer. I know they are all excited to be together again with our parents and June's parents. What a reunion that must have been. I can almost hear them singing now.

God provided Jean Brown to "sister" me even before my sister and June went to heaven, because June lived in Seattle, Washington, Elaine lived in Baton Rouge, Louisiana, and Jean still lived in Fullerton, close to me. She had traveled with Larry and me to visit June and Jim in Washington, and several times to Baton Rouge to visit my sister Elaine and husband Joe Luizzo and their family. She had also traveled with us to several other places.

Jean often comes and stays a few days with us in our home in Yucaipa. We play dominoes, cards, go out to dinner and/or a movie. We have a great time together.

We are so thankful for friends like Jean, who we can have fun with, pray with, cry with, and express freely any personal and/or serious concerns.

Another "forever friend" is Jean (Fancher) Stafford. We have been friends since junior high. Jean is a year younger, so we were together more during high school at church functions and outings. I can always count on Jean to attend any family get together or celebration. She is like a younger sister to me. We celebrate our birthdays together every year at Knott's Berry Farm's Chicken Dinner Restaurant, where we worked as teenagers. We worked in teams of two, but Jean and I were not teamed up together. However,

God blessed me with another "forever friend" to partner with me. Her name is Patti. Jean and Patti were next door neighbors growing up. The three of us try to get together once a year. We usually meet at Patti's lovely home, and then go to lunch and catch up on all that has happened in our lives during the past year. I am so thankful to God for our friends of many years.

New Friends also Blessed Our Lives

Besides our old-time friends, God has brought cherished new friends into Larry's and my life. These special people uplift, comfort, and love us, and we are grateful. It is so important not to minimize the impact good friends bring into our lives, especially during times of crises.

One of those times occurred in Fullerton. I had a good neighbor, Reta Hutchins. Reta and her husband, Tom, had two little boys, Tim and Scott, with whom Todd loved to play. One day I noticed Todd had a rash. I was pregnant with Trent, our youngest son, and I knew it was important to get Todd to the doctor not only for him, but I realized there was a danger if I got measles while pregnant.

I had just laid our baby daughter Jill down for her nap. I called Reta to see if she could baby sit her so I wouldn't have to wake her. Reta wasn't home. I kept checking her driveway to see if she had returned home, but no. Just as I was reaching down in the crib to pick Jill up, Reta "popped" in the door and said, "Joyce do you need me to babysit?"

I said, "How did you know?" I had been saying something like, *"Lord, please have Reta get home before I have to leave."*

Reta said, "Well, I was shopping in La Habra at the mall, and I just kept hearing, 'Go home, Joyce needs you!'" That was the first time I had experienced the working of the Holy Spirit in such a dramatic way. Though I did not understand the Holy Spirit or how He operated at that time, I knew God had relayed the message to Reta.

When we moved to Yucaipa, we experienced the true meaning of the *"gift of hospitality."* Romans 12: 6, 13 (NASB) says, *"And since we have gifts that differ according to the grace given to us, let each exercise them accordingly: ...contributing to the needs of the saints, practicing hospitality."*

Harry and Alene Whitt invited us to their lovely home after church one Sunday. Alene had prepared homemade pie and coffee to welcome us to the church family. I learned later she always prepared pies and froze them so they could be baked whenever new people came to church.

She was a great friend, and I admired her ability to organize everything so well. Alene has since gone to be with the Lord after a long battle with cancer. Her husband,

Harry, is still our dear friend. He is always there when we need him. He has been a real support in our efforts with Todd. I cannot think of one time he did not come to our rescue with a cheerful, willing heart, truly desiring to be of help.

We also met Bob and JoAnn Kraut who became our close friends. The day Todd trashed the house, they came as soon as they heard to support us. Bob offered to help clean up, but Larry was still having some trouble with pride and refused out of embarrassment. I actually think by the look on Bob's face that Larry hurt Bob's feelings.

Proverbs 16:18 (NASB) says, *"Pride goes before destruction and a haughty spirit before stumbling."*

When friends sincerely offer to help in a crisis situation, we need to let them.

I'm sure our bond of friendship would have flourished and grown deeper had we let them help us. Prov. 17: 17 (AMP) says, *"A Friend loves at all Times."*

Another forever friend was Archie Huff. I considered her my spiritual mother; she supplied me with much spiritual food. She was also like a physical mother to Larry and me, and like a grandmother to our children. She took care of Todd several times and gave him odd jobs around her house. She also wrote letters of recommendation to Pepperdine University when Jill and Trent were ready to apply there for college.

When Jill went with Pepperdine students to Italy for a school year, Archie gave her money for the Euro-rail. She was always there to help, even financially.

Friends Can Help You Cope

Archie had a friend, Joyce Megas, who also became my special friend. The three of us started meeting every week for lunch, and God used Joyce to provide cassette tapes that built my faith and helped me cope with the turmoil going on in our family. Larry and I would play the tapes she gave us on our vacations and also on short trips in the car. These tapes helped us tremendously when there were problems with Todd. Those scriptures helped to calm the storms raging in our souls.

Christian Friends Can Inspire You and Teach You

Mary Gauer is like a younger sister to me. She has three children, two of which are handicapped. Mary has many trials of her own, having one son with a club foot that had to be amputated so he has an artificial leg, and her oldest daughter has cerebral palsy and epilepsy.

Mary was such an inspiration to me. Through her I learned how to hear from God. I always knew God spoke to us through His Word, but I did not give God the glory for the good things He did through me and others.

For example:

Mary said, "The Lord told me to take some groceries to a friend in need."

I said, "Mary, how do you know God told you to do that? Do you hear an audible voice?"

She said, "No, it's a thought."

I said, "Then how do you know it's God?"

She said, very simply, "Well, **I** would never think of that!"

James 1:17 (HCSB) says, *"Every generous act and every perfect gift is from above, coming down from the Father."*

She explained further, "When I went to the store, I thought, 'Now what should I get her, Lord?' The first thought that came to my mind was liver."

She said, "I was so surprised that I said right out loud, '*LIVER!*' Embarrassing myself, but I bought the liver. When I got to my friend's house, my friend said she was so amazed I had bought liver. She said the doctor had told her to eat liver two times a week because she was so anemic." Mary and I had a good laugh that she had said "liver" right out loud in the store.

Mary taught me an important principle on hearing from God. That is to never give myself credit for good deeds. I needed to give God the glory for those ideas.

Forever Friends

I no longer want say, "I took food over to a friend, or I visited a sick friend." I try to do as Mary does, and say, "The Lord told me to take food to a friend," or "The Lord put on my heart that I needed to visit my sick friend."

These wonderful friends loved us unconditionally and supported us and taught us so many things about the God kind of love.

Each of these friends contributed to Todd's well-being either directly or indirectly. Directly when interacting with him personally. Indirectly by praying, sympathizing, comforting, and/or encouraging us. They were all instrumental in our life.

They enabled us to grow stronger as Christians, which in turn helped us to cope with situations involving our son. Larry and I cherish these *gifts* we have received from our Father in heaven.

We have several new friends now. Diane Wood who was a teacher of the Bible and health in her home and at church. We had many fun times playing cards and eating out with her and her husband Bill, who recently went to be with the Lord.

Church friends Joyce and Ken Parrah, who we loved playing cards with and attending Bible class at Diane and Bill's. Joyce also attended Diane's health class with me.

Bob and Barbie are wonderful neighbors God provided for us. We could not have gotten through the last two or three years without their physical and emotional help. Also, another neighbor Loree and husband Jack, always bring us a delicious yeast pastry every Christmas.

We now have some new neighbors, Irmgart and her husband. They have so graciously offered help if we need anything. I did ask Irmgart to help me with computer problems. She also offered to type two chapters of this book that had somehow gotten deleted. We are eternally grateful to God for our forever Friends.

O Gracious Father,
Only You could have provided such friends.
Help us always to be mindful of their contributions to our lives.
Thank You.

In Jesus name,
Amen

Chapter 7

DISCOVERING THE "ABBA" FATHER

... you have received a spirit of adoption as sons by which we cry out, "Abba" Father!

— Rom. 8:15, NASB

The apostle Paul, known at the time as Saul, cried out as he was on the road to Damascus, *"Who art thou Lord?"* (Acts 9:5, NASB). Jesus had to literally knock Saul to the ground for him to realize who He was. Saul's heart was right, but his theology was wrong. Many of us are like that today. Not only can we misunderstand who Jesus is, we may never have met the "Abba" Father either! *Abba* in our language is Daddy. God desires for us to know Him as Daddy, to show the intimate relationship He wants to have with us.

Sometimes the Father has to knock us to the ground so to speak or use our difficult circumstances to wake us up as to who He is. Like Saul, I needed a wake-up call. I know my heart was right, but my attitude was wrong. I wanted to be a good wife and mother. I wanted my children to be completely devoted to God, which was all well and good.

In searching the motives of my heart, I found pride to be part of the reason I wanted them to be great in the kingdom of God. So, we as parents would look good and people would admire us and our family. That bit of pride overrode all the other reasons and purposes. I tried to make things perfect or right in my own strength.

I was struggling with three teenagers and also going through menopause. Our house was in shambles with Todd totally out of control. I soon was humbled before God.

Disciplining hurts, but I am eternally grateful because through it all I developed a closer relationship with the Father as my "Abba" Father.

He used these difficulties and circumstances to "whip" me into shape. I'm still being shaped, but I learned a lot about myself while being stripped of the things I thought were so important. Heb. 12:6, 10 (NASB) says, *"For those whom the Lord loves He disciplines and He scourges every son whom He receives. It is for discipline that you endure. ...He disciplines us for our good, that we may share His holiness."*

God did not suddenly become my Abba Father just because I discovered that this was who He was. He has been my Abba Father my whole life. He is everyone's who desires Him to be. Though He did some very special things for me after my earthly father died. I was eleven, I just took all the things God did for granted thinking it was just life.

One day as I thought about this, I realized all the times God saved me from many experiences where I could have been in grave danger. But I wasn't really aware of His

DISCOVERING THE "ABBA" FATHER

protection at the time. One particular incident stands out, and I will share it with you. "Abba" Father protected me in such a surprising way.

I was fourteen and had gone to a party with some friends. When we got to the house of the person having the party, there were no adults present. The liquor cabinet was open for the kids to drink whatever they wanted and as much as they wanted. The kids were smoking and dancing and doing only God knows what in the bedrooms.

Since I didn't smoke or drink or do whatever else the kids were doing, I was just standing in the living room by a bedroom doorway. I was feeling very uncomfortable and wishing I hadn't come. A *very cute boy* with blonde curly hair came in the front door. He was dressed in Levi's and wearing no shirt as it *was* a very hot night. He came up to me and rested his arm on the doorway over me and, looking down at me, said, "What are you doing here?"

I replied, "I came with my friends."

Then he said, "You don't belong here, why you don't let me take you home?"

So, I went with him, and he took me straight home just as he promised. Normally, I would never have gone anywhere with a stranger, but I did go with him. Funny thing is, I cannot remember any conversation, where I lived, or anything for that matter from the time I got in the car until I was at my house. I got out of the car, thanked him, and then realize I hadn't even asked his name. I turned around to try and hail him but neither he nor the car were anywhere in sight. The next day I asked my friends who the stranger was, and no one knew who he was either. They said they thought he was *my* friend. No one ever saw him again. One day, I believed God spoke to my heart and said He had sent the angel to rescue me from that party situation when I was a teenager.

This wonderful "Daddy" Father also gave me an example of His continued watchful care and powerful love for me and my husband. It came years later, on our twenty-fourth wedding anniversary through our daughter, Jill, and again on our twenty-fifth wedding anniversary from each of our children. Children are truly a *gift* from God.

For our twenty-fourth anniversary, thirteen-year-old Jill carved out on a piece of wood, *"LOVE NEVERS FAILS."* She painted flowers on it and a bright yellow sun in the corner. God used that little block of wood I had set on the fire screen edge by the fireplace to remind me of His *agape* love. There were times I would not have made it through the day if it weren't for that little reminder.

Because I am updating this manuscript after having put it aside for several years, I have an amazing story about this little block of wood in my published memoir (*From Little Pauper Girl to Princess Bride Forever After*). Then the following year our children gave us our silver anniversary party. We were so surprised because Todd was just seventeen, Jill fourteen, and Trent twelve.

DISCOVERING THE "ABBA" FATHER

I want to share with you some of the thoughtful things each of them did on our day that was special. Todd was so helpful to Larry in the yard. The party place was a surprise, so for all we knew, it could have been at our house. Todd had not gotten around to vacuuming his room when his grandpa and wife, Wilma, showed up early. Todd came to me and said, "Mom is it all right if I go ahead and vacuum my room even though Grandpa and Wilma are here?" I said sure, and he really did do a nice job on his room.

Jill began planning the party two years beforehand. What amazed us was that she had been saving some of her allowance and babysitting money since she was twelve. For a wedding anniversary gift, Jill bought us a twenty-fifth wedding anniversary album.

In it, she wrote: "August 26, 1982

Dearest Father and Mother,

I love you both so very much. I wanted to get you this album, because it fit you so well. The love you share is so encouraging to me, and to everyone around you.

Twenty-five years is quite a long time. This day and age, it's so hard for families to survive, but through your example I see that with God, a family can be one in love.

The next twenty-five will even be better, for I can see you both are growing in Christ, and in the Spirit, and in love.

Miraculously My Own

I hope you enjoy this book, and may it always bring memories of love.

God Bless You both,

Love you,

Jill Elaine" (Age 14)

Trent, our youngest, helped with the party by making signs for parking. He had to wait for our long-time friend, Jean Brown, to come from Fullerton; she came early to help Trent place the signs so we wouldn't know where they were being placed.

The kids had their grandpa and his wife, Wilma, drive us to the party with our eyes closed until we got to the door of the place. Grandpa drove around and around, but we actually ended up right across the street from our house at our neighbors'--Mary Lou and Pete Malbovich--home. Their daughter, Meah, swam on the swim team with our kids. She was like another daughter to us. Meah helped our kids plan and decorate for the party. Her family offered their home and took pictures. They were a great help before, during, and after the party.

Larry and I will always remember the lovely day that our children blessed and honored us. We were so surprised

DISCOVERING THE "ABBA" FATHER

at their thoughtfulness at such young ages. I know our "Abba" Father put those thoughts into their hearts because, as God's Word says in James 1:17 (HCBS), *"Every generous act and every perfect gift is from God."*

Our anniversary party was the most "generous act" and "perfect gift" our children could have given us. Their thoughtfulness blessed and humbled me to receive such a gift. After reading and digesting the scripture in James 1:17, I realized God had instigated the thought. I was drawn to a closer relationship and deeper love for my Abba Father. What a great Abba Father! Now I know He is always with me and daily helps me. It is my desire to stay close to Him and continually seek and follow His plan for my life.

It is impossible to talk about God without speaking of His love, for God is love; He doesn't just have love. He *is* love, and real love, as the little block of wood reminds us that *"love never fails "*(See, I Cor. 13:8a). I may never comprehend the height, depth, and breadth of God's love, but I know I'm at least learning and headed in the right direction.

Each person of the Godhead has shown they are "love" in their own way. The "Abba" Father loved us so much that He sent His Son to die for us. Jesus willingly came and died on the cross for us since we could not pay for our sins. Then Jesus sent His Spirit, the Holy Spirit, who dwells in us, comforts and guides us into all truth! Acts 1:8 tells us that through the Spirit we receive *power* to fight the battles we face in life, and the indwelling Spirit keeps us from sinning. (See I John 3:9.)

I didn't know much about the Holy Spirit before our problems started with Todd. I envisioned some kind of ghost-like vapor floating around in the atmosphere. I knew He was the inspiration for the writers of the Bible, which was about all I really understood about Him. That was sad because I was raised in a Bible-based church all my life, and I thought I really knew the Word. I even taught Bible classes! His Word did help me to know where to go as the pressure mounted with Todd. I would retreat to my bedroom and study God's Word, pray, and listen to the tapes that Joyce Megas had given me.

I found when I took a step toward Abba Father, He would take at least two steps toward me.

> *And because you are sons, God has sent forth the Spirit of His Son into your hearts, crying Abba Father Wherefore, thou art no more a servant but a son and if a son, then an heir of God, through Christ.*
>
> — Gal. 4:6-7, KJV

Jesus explained in John 14:21 (NASB) how we can know if we love Him. It's a marvelous promise. He said,

> *He who has my commandments and keeps them, he it is who loves me, and he who loves me shall*

DISCOVERING THE "ABBA" FATHER

be loved by my Father and I will love him and disclose myself to him.

— John 14:21, NASB

I asked myself, *what is the "condition" in order for me to receive that promise?*

Was I keeping God's commandments--the most important Commandment, to love God with my whole heart, and soul, and mind? (See Matt. 22:37-40)

Did I love my neighbor as myself? I felt like a complete failure as a wife and mother as everything seemed to be falling apart. Neither was I being a very good friend. I was so wrapped up in our family's problems. I actually was not able to love my neighbor, because I didn't love myself.

I had to meditate on God's love for me until I could convince myself that I must be worth loving if God said He love me. Through prayer and earnest desire to know Him, His presence became so real. I knew He loved me, and I could trust Him and totally rely on Him for every need. Now I was able to love and care for people in need. This had become a real desire of my heart. My most important desire was to prove my love to Todd.

Miraculously My Own

My loving Abba Father,

During those times when I felt the need to retreat to my bedroom,

I felt as though I could crawl upon Your lap, feeling safe the same way

I did on my earthly father's lap. Knowing I was blessed to have an earthly

father I could trust made it easier to love and trust You Abba Father.

Now You, "Abba," heavenly Daddy, comfort me. You let me know everything

will be all right, no matter how strong the forces of wickedness and evil are

that come to attack our family.

Thank You, Abba
, In Jesus name,
Amen.

Chapter 8

DARK FORCES OF EVIL

*Giving thanks unto the Father **Who** hath delivered us from the power of darkness and hath translated us into the Kingdom of His dear Son.*

— Col. 1:12, 13, KJV

Experiencing the trials, I talk about in this book not only drew me closer to God, but it forced me to learn more about Satan and his demonic world. John 10:10 (AMP) informs us that, *"The thief comes only in order to steal, and kill, and destroy."* (The thief is in reference to Satan). In contrast, Jesus said, *"I came that they may have life, and have it in abundance (to the full, till it over flows)"* (John 10:10, AMP).

I had to face the fact that Satan and his demonic power was real. I had always believed that if something was spiritual, it had to be good!

When you ask God for wisdom, expect to learn all of the truth, both good and evil. He loves us and wants us to be able to discern between what is spiritually good and spiritually evil.

Through some in-depth study of the Scripture and my

personal experience of fighting Satan as he tormented Todd, it became evident to me that there was godly spirits and also demonic spirits in the spirit world. Some of Satan's activities were deceptive, but some are real and can be true, though that does not make them right and/or good!

I discovered the Bible has scriptures to help us keep our mind straight on what are Godly spirits and what are demonic. I have listed two examples of satanic activities that are common today, first in a deceptive way and then in a factual way.

One thing I have discovered is that Satan deceives people into believing that they had a previous life. He can use hypnosis because a person's mind is open to suggestions.

Demons can tell a person truthful thing that happened years before that they were born.

They can relate times, places, and events that actually happened, and describe everything down to the most minute detail, which convinces the person and others that they truly did have a previous life. Since demons are spirits, it is no big mystery that they can implant in a person's mind things that happened centuries before. However, the Bible says, in Heb. 9:27 (KJV) that, "*It is appointed unto men once to die, but after this the judgment.*" This scripture explains that people have only one life. The following is another example of satanic activity that is very prevalent today.

DARK FORCES OF EVIL

Mediums, Witches, Warlocks (and the Like)

Mediums allow demon spirits to inhabit their bodies. The mediums are then able to reveal all kinds of things to unsuspecting persons who don't know God. What they do <u>is real.</u> That is why God warns us to not have anything to do with them. He gives many examples. The following Bible story makes the point very clear.

Witches have the ability to bring up dead relatives or others with whom people want to communicate. The Bible verifies this ability in I Samuel 28: 7-25 (MSG). The witch of Endor brought Samuel, the prophet, up from the dead. King Saul sought her out for answers because God was no longer with him. Saul had been disobedient to God. When Saul saw *"the Philistines had mustered their troops… he shook in his boots, scared to death"* (I Samuel 28: 4-5, MSG).

> *Saul prayed to God, but God didn't answer. So, Saul ordered his officials, find me someone who could call up spirits so I may go and seek counsel from those spirits. His servants said, "There is a witch at Endor."*
>
> — I Samuel 28, MSG

Saul put on different clothes to disguise himself and took two men with him and went under the cover of night to the woman. He said to the witch, *"I want you to consult a ghost for me. Call up the person I name"* (I Sam. 28, MSG).

Miraculously My Own

The woman said, *"Just hold on now! You know what Saul did, how he swept the country clean of mediums why are you trying to trap me and get me killed?"* (I Sam. 28, MSG).

Saul swore she would not get in trouble for this. So, the woman said, *"So whom do you want me to bring up?"* (I Sam. 28, MSG). Saul had the medium (Witch of Endor) conjure up the prophet Samuel, who had died. Saul just had to know what was going to happen to him.

> *When the woman saw Samuel, she cried out loudly to Saul, "Why did you lie to me? You're Saul!"*
>
> *The King told her, "You have nothing to fear.... but what do you see?"*
>
> *"I see a spirit ascending from the underground."*
>
> *"And what does he look like?" Saul asked.*
>
> *"An old man ascending, robed like a priest."*
>
> *Saul knew it was Samuel. He fell down, face to the ground, and worshiped.*

DARK FORCES OF EVIL

> *Samuel said to Saul, "Why have you disturbed me by calling me up?"*
>
> *Saul said, "Because I am in deep trouble, The Philistines are making war against me and God has deserted me. He doesn't answer me anymore, either by prophet or by dream. So, I'm calling on you to tell me what to do."*
>
> *"Why ask me?" said Samuel. "God has turned away from you and is now on the side of your neighbor. God has done exactly what he told you through me – ripped the kingdom right out of your hands and given it to your neighbor It's because you did not obey God... that*
>
> *God does to you what He is doing today. Worse yet, God is turning Israel, along with you over to the Philistines. Tomorrow you and your sons will be with me. And, yes, indeed, God is giving Israel's army up to the philistines."*
>
> — I Sam. 28, MSG

Saul fell to the ground, terrified by Samuel's words. There wasn't any strength left in him. He hadn't eaten anything all day and all night. The Witch realized he was in deep shock and said to him,

> *"Listen to me. I did what you asked me to do, put my life in your hands in doing it, carried out your instructions to the letter. It's your turn to*

> *do what I tell you. Let me give you some food. Eat it. It will give you strength so you can get on your way." He refused saying, "I'm not eating anything."*
>
> — I Samuel 28: 7-25, MSG

His servants also urged him, and he gave in to their pleas. After dining well, they got up from the table and were on their way the same night. See I Samuel 28: 23-25 (MSG).

> *The Philistines made war on Israel... [They killed Saul's three sons.] The battle was hot and heavy around Saul. The archers got in his range and wounded Saul badly. Saul said to his weapon bearer, "Draw your sword and put me out of my misery, lest these pagan pigs come and make a game out of killing me." But his weapon bearer wouldn't do it. He was terrified. So, Saul took the sword himself and fell on it. When the weapon bearer saw that Saul was dead, he too fell on his sword. So, Saul, his three sons, and his weapon bearer ---the men closest to him ---died together that day."*
>
> — Samuel 31: 1-6, MSG

This story not only lets us know we are not to seek out people controlled by Satan and the occult; it also lets us know if we do find out and learn the future, it may not be what we want to hear! In these two examples, God warns us not to have anything to do with any occult activity. We only need God's Holy Spirit to guide us. See Deut. 18:10, 11- II Kings 21:6, The New Testament Acts 19: 11-16.

Demonic Influences

I have noticed that children who are extremely handicapped, either physically and/or mentally, usually receive a lot of attention, help, and love. On the other hand, children like Todd who do not have a visible disability may seem as though they are being purposely odd or different, even rebellious. In response, other children and even some adults, can be intolerant even to the point of disdaining the handicapped individual. Todd experienced this type of reaction from some of his peers and, many times, adults. Satan especially targets the slightly handicapped, bombarding them with thoughts of how unworthy they are of love and attention. Satan said things to Todd like, "God doesn't love you, look how He made you."

Todd actually asked me one day, "Why did God make me like this?" Satan might have said, "Your natural parents didn't love you; they gave you away." Todd remarked one day that he wondered at times what had happened to the lady who grew him.

Another thing Satan might implant in an adopted child's mind is that your adoptive parents love their biological children more than you. Satan did put this thought in Todd's mind because, as I mentioned in a previous chapter, he made the comment that because he was adopted, he was different from us. He said, "I have different *germs* so I cannot hug or kiss you."

I laughed and said, "We all have the same germs, Todd. It's *genes* that are different not germs!" So, I told him, "We love you just the same, and it's okay to hug and kiss us."

Satan tormented Todd with these thoughts and more, which contributed to Todd's low self-esteem and lack of self-worth.

I observed my sweet boy become so frustrated that he became like a monster! I tried to *make* him act right. There were times he would have unprovoked anger and might start cussing at me or saying things to upset me.

Instead of using this time to pray with him, I would get angry right back, causing him to feel justified in tearing up the house in some fashion. I would try to stop him from getting violent, and we actually became monster against monster. Sometimes it even became a hair pulling contest!

Jesus gives us the authority to rebuke Satan and his influence in the name of Jesus. Larry and I needed to learn how to fight Satan.

Learning to Fight Demonic Influences and Tear Down Strongholds

I was fighting a spiritual battle in the power of the flesh. No one can win a spiritual battle without spiritual weapons.

DARK FORCES OF EVIL

The Word of God says in II Cor. 10: 3-5 (HCSB):

> *Although we are walking in the flesh, we do not wage war in a fleshly way, since the weapons of our warfare are not fleshly, but are powerful through God for the demolitions of strongholds. We demolish arguments and every high-minded thing that is raised up against the knowledge of God, taking every thought captive to the obedience of Christ.*
>
> — II Cor. 10:3-5, HCSB

Spiritual weapons are listed and the instruction on how to use them in

Eph.6:11-15 (HCSB). In addition, Ephesians says:

> *In every situation take the shield of faith and with it you will be able to extinguish the flaming arrows of the evil one. Take the helmet of salvation and the sword of the Spirit, which is the Word of God.*
>
> — Ephesians 6:16-17, (HCSB)

There were times when I saw Todd's eyes become piercing and beady. I recall one time in particular. I was walking past him as he was looking out from the bathroom at me into the dark hall. He started cursing at me using all kinds of foul language. I looked at him and I saw his pupils go from wide open to pinpoint in size.

Later, I related this phenomenon to my daughter, Jill. I made the comment, "I wonder why Todd's pupils went from wide open to pinpoint when he looked at me, since it was so dark in the hall?"

Jill responded, "Well, think about it, Mom, isn't Jesus light, and isn't Jesus living in you?"

When Satan or a demon would enter Todd's thoughts and he would start acting like he did in the bathroom that day and when my faith was weak, I would leave the house. If I tried to confront him in my fearful condition, he would get violent, and continue his rage, knock holes in the walls and doors and smash anything in sight.

Christians can be obsessed of the devil when we, as Eph. 4:27 (NASB) says, "give the devil an opportunity." Todd would in some way, "give the devil an opportunity."

The Bible says that believers are to do all that Jesus taught His apostles to do (Matt.28:18-20). Therefore, if you are put in a position as I was with Todd, it is important to be prepared to confront Satan and/or his demons and to do it in faith.

I began studying how Jesus handled demons (Mark 16: 15-18). When I learned to rebuke Satan, telling him in the name of Jesus to leave Todd alone, Satan would leave, and Todd would be all right for a while. It was really very strange to realize I was actually speaking to the devil and/or a demon.

When Jesus comes, He will set things right. Until then Satan will always return when we least expect him and at our weakest moment.

DARK FORCES OF EVIL

If I was not able to let the anointing of Jesus work through me and I tried to confront Todd, he would really come after me in a violent rage. I remembered the story in the Bible of the sons of Sceva who tried to use the name of Jesus without His anointing to do so in Acts, 19: 11 – 16 (MSG). This is the story:

> *"God did powerful things through Paul, things quite out of the ordinary. The word got around and people started taking pieces of clothing – handkerchiefs and scarves and the like – that had touched Paul's skin and then touching the sick with them. The touch did it – they were healed and whole.*
>
> *"Some itinerant Jewish exorcists who happened to be in town at the time tried their hand at what they assumed to be Paul's game. They pronounced the name of the Master Jesus over victims of evil spirits, saying, "I command you by the Jesus preached by Paul!"*
>
> *"The seven sons of a certain Sceva, a Jewish High priest, were trying to do this on a man when the evil spirit talked back:" "I know Jesus and I've heard of Paul but who are you?" "Then the possessed man went berserk – jumped the exorcists, beat them up, and tore off their clothes. Naked and bloody, they got away as best they could."*

"It was soon news all over Ephesus among both Jews and Greeks. The realization spread that God was in and behind this. Curiosiy about Paul developed into reverence for the Master Jesus.

Many of those who thus believed came out of the closet and made a clean break with their secret sorceries. All kinds of witches and warlocks came out of the woodwork with their books of spells and incantations and made a huge bonfire of them. Someone estimated their worth at fifty thousand silver coins.

It became evident that the Word of Jesus was now sovereign and prevailed in Ephesus."

— Acts 19: 11 – 16, MSG

Therefore, I learned I could not be fearful. I had to have the anointing of Jesus to rebuke Satan or I had the very same reaction from the evil spirits as the sons of Sceva did.

One time my sister Elaine and her family came to visit. Elaine was aware of the way Satan worked on Todd. Todd held a special place in her heart, as all three of her children are also adopted.

Barbara and Jon Whan, long-time friends of ours, invited us all over for dinner. Todd loved the Whans and wanted to go with us. However, his old habit of stalling when he had to be at a certain place at a certain time returned. He'd comb his hair over and over, wash his hands, get a drink, anything to stall and be in control of the situation. Some months before, the Lord spoke to my heart that stalling was Todd's way of being in control. He instructed me to tell him that he was to be in the car before anyone else or we were to leave him. I was to give him ample time to get ready. It had been working great, but this time he went back to his old way.

I knew Satan was back trying all our patience. Todd said, "Oh, you can wait!"

We said "No! Dinner would not wait, and it was not polite to be late for a dinner invitation."

Todd had also been learning how demons were using him and preventing him, if he allowed them to, from ever enjoying himself. Just the same, he continued to stall.

Satan was aware that we all wanted Todd to go and enjoy the family and friends. Finally, my sister and I went to Todd, put our arms around him, held him tight and said, "Todd! Help us fight! Rebuke Satan's power over you." He suddenly realized what was happening and he said, "Satan, I rebuke you, get away from me, in the name of Jesus." Raising his fist toward heaven, he shouted, "King of Kings and Lord of Lords!" Elaine and I were still holding Todd, and he just went limp in our arms and wept. Then he was just fine. He went to dinner with us immediately, and we had a great time.

Todd was our wonderful "normal" son again, he was

free. For a couple of days, he was able to get up in the morning and dress quickly. My sister and brother-in-law, Joe, commented on the change in Todd. It was good to see him get up and get ready quickly.

Then one morning he went to do some "odd jobs" with a friend. As I mentioned before Satan always comes back at a more opportune time (see Luke 4:13). So, Todd became rebellious again, and then the devil would work on Larry-- "I'm his father and he *will* do as I say!" Consequently, they had many knock-down and drag-outs.

Larry finally realized Satan was pitting him and Todd against each other. When Larry began to take authority as head of the family and submitted to God and stood against Satan with the Word of God, Satan and all his demons had to leave.

When Jesus went to heaven, He gave us authority to use His name. He also sent His Holy Spirit to enable us to carry on His work (see Cor. 3:16, 17). When husbands and fathers exercise their authority over demonic activities, Satan recognizes that headship. James 4:7 tells us he and his demons must flee in terror.

Quoting from Jack Deere's book, on Kingdom Power (pg. 225) he says:

Surprised by the Power of the Spirit

Jesus brought an authority over demons that had never been seen or heard of before (cf. Mark 1:27).

Jesus himself said, "But if I drive out demons by the Spirit of God, then the Spirit of God has come upon you." (Matthew 12:28)

After all, it would be a very hallow assertion to proclaim that the rule of God has come and not be able to cast out the demonic enemies of God's rule. The power to cast out demons is not simply a sign that the kingdom is here, but an essential part of the rule of God For;" Jesus came to destroy the works of the devil." (I John 3:8) Among other things, the devil employs supernatural power to blind the minds of unbelievers (II Corinthians, 4:2-6), to hold people in bondage through the fear of death (Hebrews 2:14-15), to cause physical illness (Luke 8:26-39), and ultimately to cause demons to enter and dwell in a person.

(Matthew 12:45; cf.) (Judas in, John 13:27). These are some of the works of the devil that Jesus came to destroy. The works of the devil cannot be destroyed by mere human power. (Kingdom Power)

Larry and I, as do all believers, have authority to cast out demons because the Holy Spirit lives in us and He does the work. However, in a family, the "headship" position carries greater and more effective results (see Mark 16: 15 – 18).

Satan's plan was to get us to doubt God's Word and power. When we doubted, Satan was able to deceive us. It gave him the foothold he needed to get us to submit to his will. He changed the truth just enough to plant seeds of doubt in our hearts and minds. That was how Satan got Eve to eat the fruit of the tree of the knowledge of good and evil. He still evidently uses those same tactics today.

Satan's main focus is the Christian home because it is a mini-church, and the church is Christ's body. If Satan could tear our family apart, it would be his greatest triumph, as it would ruin our mini-church witness. God's Word becomes powerless and of little effect. Satan is our enemy. Not Larry, me, Todd, Jill, Trent, or any of our friends. Eph. 6:12 reminded us that our fight is *not* against flesh and blood.

Larry and I became the devil's tool when we would lash out at each other or the children (Prov. 18: 21, James, 3: 6). Satan, knowing our weaknesses, would attack whenever we let our guard down.

Jesus gave us the Holy Spirit so we would not sin. I John 5: 18 (NASB) says,

> *"We know that no one who is born of God sins. He who is born of God keeps him and the evil*

one does not touch him."

You say, "WAIT A MINUTE!" You mean we are not born again if we sin? Well, yes, if we continue to live in sin. Jesus through His blood keeps us, and Satan cannot touch us as long as we have a repentant heart and our desire is to live for Jesus and continue to learn obedience. I might add here that we may have to learn obedience through the things that we suffer.

Understanding that "anger" is actually fear, hurt, and/or frustration helped me begin to overcome anger. Larry and I began spending more personal time with the

Lord. Our faith grew stronger as we meditated on God's Word, and we were more able to control our anger. Sin saddens the heart of the people who love us.

It becomes easier and easier not to sin as we grew in the grace and the knowledge of our Lord and Savior Jesus Christ. In His presence, we began to hate sin. Sin caused us to carry around the burden of guilt and disrespect from the ones we love. Our goal was to stay in His presence, where all sin ceased to be.

However, for our family, there were still more years of trial ahead.

Miraculously My Own

Mighty Father God,
When trials come, and we remember to ask You,
Your grace, wisdom, and strength are always available.

Thank you,

In Jesus name,
Amen

Chapter 9

More Years of Trial

Blessed is the man who perseveres under trial, because when he has stood the test, he will receive the crown of life that God has promised to those who love Him.

— James 1:12, NASB

When Todd was a young child, the pediatrician explained that there was a "short circuit" that interfered with his ability to move physically. It happened intermittently; consequently, people couldn't understand when he would stop and just stand still for a time. His brain would send messages to his body, and sometimes it would respond and sometimes it couldn't. Todd's employers would think he was just standing and goofing off. He was just standing and not doing anything because sometimes his body would not move. Todd would then purposely stand longer because he was embarrassed. He would rather people think he was doing nothing on purpose than for them to think he had a disability. I actually observed him doing this at one of his jobs.

With Todd's teen years over and many hard lessons learned through trial and error, one would think our family would have won the battle over pride and anger. However, we still were not realizing the value of praying with Todd the moment he began to act up. We really didn't want to pray. We were still trying to conquer problems with Todd by using our own power and our own strength, rather than trusting in God's.

Since Todd had dropped out of high school and was unable to hold down a job, he was so frustrated that he became harder and harder to live with. He would get mad at the drop of a hat. We were all under extreme tension every day. Our patience was being stretched so tight because of the constant violence Todd displayed if we said the wrong thing or made the wrong move.

I realized he was actually angry at himself, and the family got the brunt of it. He so wanted to work and be independent. Dealing with Todd's outbursts became very difficult. Our walls and most of our doors had holes from his anger and frustration. This went on for approximately ten years. He then began isolating himself from the family and family functions.

During the day when Todd was at home, I would stay away from the house as much as possible just to avoid confrontation.

Larry began taking Todd, now in his twenties, to the library in the mornings. He was to look for a job during the day. Larry would pick him up on his way back home from work. Eventually, Todd stopped looking for work it was just too traumatic for him. It is very difficult to describe the

More Years of Trial

next several years.

Todd started just staying in his room. He actually barricaded himself in it. He only came out to go the bathroom and eat occasionally. His hair grew long, he lost weight, his fingernails grew long, and he came out of his room less and less. I finally said, "Todd, you are not going to die in this house." I warned him that I would call family services if he didn't come out of his room and start living again. He did not believe me or care if I did, so I called family services.

Two ladies came to the house. Todd locked himself in the bathroom and would not come out. The ladies said they would have to call the police if he didn't come out. Eventually, they did have to call the police. Todd was now thirty-five. Our new neighbor happened to be the sheriff. I don't know if he received the call or just heard Todd was being a problem. He told me he wanted to be the one to come to our house (God's grace).

Larry or I hadn't met him before, but he said he knew Todd. He and Todd had visited a few times around and about our homes. Since we live in the country, we are not right next door. I was very grateful Todd knew him and that he came to the house to talk to him. He got him to come out of the bathroom. Todd was willing to go with the sheriff. The sheriff said it was mandatory that he handcuff him. I could not help but cry. The Sheriff took Todd to Ward B in San Bernardino. They tested him, and after several days, he was diagnosed with bi-polar disorder and schizophrenia. He was assigned to Burley's Board and Care Facility, where he has resided for the last thirteen years.

We praised God for finding a good home for Todd, and though it was a very difficult transition, he eventually began to feel like it was his home. We are continuing to thank God for answering our prayer that Todd is in an appropriate place with Mrs. Burley, who understands and truly cares about his special needs.

Gracious Father in heaven,
Though there were more years of trial,
our love for one another grew
as we persevered and endured each trial.
Help us to continue to look
to you for strength.
We thank You and praise You, Father,
for all You do, have done, and will do in the future, for all of us.

In Jesus name,
Amen

Chapter 10

Perseverance and Endurance under Trial

(A Love Producer)

> *We exalt in hope of the glory of God. And not only this, but we also Exalt in our tribulation, knowing that tribulation brings about perseverance.*
>
> — **Romans 5: 2b, 3, NASB**

Even though Todd was out of the house and in a good home, we still needed to look at our lives and prayerfully ask God what we could have done to prevent all the hurt and violence.

In Eph. 6:4, God instructs us not to provoke our children to wrath. We did not provoke Todd intentionally. I would realize after the fact we were unintentionally doing just that. I remember thinking to myself, "Why did I say that?" Had I thought before I spoke and had used some self-control, I could have avoided many altercations. I finally realized my words were many times provoking Todd to anger.

In the natural realm, I believe we did all we could. That was the problem, and the reason I felt the need to write this book. We were living more in the natural or fleshly realm than in the supernatural or spiritual realm.

God informed Larry and me in His Word that if we will, *"Walk in the Spirit we will not fulfill the lust of the flesh"* (Gal. 5:16, NKJV)

In verses 19 and 20 I read what the works of the flesh are. In verse 20, it lists the word "variance," which is defined as, discord, conflict, factions, quarrels, fights, contention and strife. These were all the ways we reacted to Todd's defiance and rebellion. Gal. 5: 21 (KJV) warns us *those that do such things shall not inherit the kingdom of God*! WOW that was a scary thought! We really needed the fruit of the Spirit in our home.

Gal. 5: 22 (KJV) says, when we develop the fruit of the Spirit--*love, joy, peace, long suffering, gentleness, goodness, faith, meekness, and temperance--we will avoid the works of the flesh*. We needed to remember it took a while for fruit to develop, so we would not get discouraged or feel overwhelmed, thinking we would never be able to bear all those fruits. I had to realize no tree produces its fruit overnight, but since we have received Jesus into our hearts, we have the seeds in our spirit. We knew we had to work on the fruit of love, feed, and water it, and all the other fruits would follow in time.

I didn't realize the importance of the fruit of the Spirit in order to experience the abundant life Jesus promised. Love is the first fruit mentioned as fruit of the Spirit; it is also, the first commandment. In Mark 12: 29-30, Jesus was asked, *"Which is the greatest commandment?"*

He said, *"This is the most important one…You shall love the Lord your God with all your heart, and with all your soul, and with all your mind, and with all your strength"* (Mark 12: 29-30, NASB).

So, I discovered our love walk would produce the precious fruit of the Spirit our family so desperately needed. I memorized the fruit of the Spirit as if memorizing them would make them grow in my heart! Well, that did plant the seeds, but those seeds certainly needed lots of cultivating and care.

Larry and I needed to know something that would actually produce love in and for our family. To our surprise, we found all those trials that required *endurance and perseverance* were the keys that helped us in developing a more humble, loving, and compassionate attitude. We learned to pray with Todd when he was out of control.

Instead of an angry response to his outbursts, we prayed with compassion for him.

Because of the daily conflict in our home, our family did go to counseling. One was with a Christian psychologist, one was not, and both proved to be unfruitful. Psychologists that are recommended by a good friend or pastor will give scriptures to feed on that could have helped our family. Todd's problems affected our entire family. Only God has the answers when you are in a spiritual battle.

I will qualify this statement by saying some may find help from non-Christian counseling, depending on the particular need. However, when a family is so steeped in anger as ours, that family needs the working and help of the Holy Spirit to pull them out.

I also might add that we found not all councilors that are Christian will have the training and/or background to be of help in a given situation. Therefore, we needed the guidance of the Holy Spirit to choose the right counselor. However, we did not yet know how to listen to the Spirit's guidance.

Larry and I were still reeling from all that had transpired with Todd--his barricading himself in his room and soon to move out to Burley's Board and Care Facility--when we received word that Larry's mom had a stroke.

Larry's brother Don and wife Donna lived closer to Mom in Westminster, California. They had cared for Mom's needs for several years. The doctor told Mom while she was in the hospital that she would not ever be able to return home. She needed assisted living. There was a beautiful assisted living place in Redlands, close to where we lived, so we moved her there. Seeing to both Mom's and Todd's needs at times was difficult.

Todd did not drive, so we took him to his doctor appointments, counseling (required by the state), and to church. He did take the bus some places.

More Years of Trial

All this came at a time when I wanted to spend more time with the Lord. The lack of time became a challenge. I could not to go off to a quiet place by myself to meditate as I had planned. Larry and I did make a decision to read the Bible and pray together daily. I also found journaling is a great faith builder. When I write my thoughts and prayers down, it is so encouraging to go back later and read them. I'm amazed at how many prayers God answered. If I had not written those thoughts down, I would never have realized His constant care and work in my life.

I learned that:

> *We also exalt in our tribulation knowing that tribulation brings about perseverance, and perseverance, proven character and proven character, hope, and hope does not disappoint because the love of God has been poured out within our hearts through the Holy Spirit, who was given us.*
>
> — Rom. 2: 7-10, Rom. 5: 3-5, NASB

What a marvelous scripture for me to meditate on. I've heard *hope* expressed as the blueprint of our faith. Our family truly needed a blueprint for our faith to be able to picture where our future as a family was headed.

The Psalmist David reminded me that my hope was in God (see Psalms 39: 7)! Therefore, through hope in God, I could see my faith was working by love, and because of that, our family was going to be fine. We learned not to worry, for God was faithful. He was always there to work things out. His grace was and always is sufficient.

I recounted the steps for us to gain hope for our life they are:

1) *Tribulation and distress,* (Romans 5: 3-5, NASB) which brings about—

2) *Perseverance.* (Romans 2: 4, 7-11, NASB)

3) *Proven Character* (Rom.5:4, NASB) helped us press through the difficulties. We could now experience—

4) *Hope in God.* Romans, 5: 4-5 (NASB) says, *"Hope does not disappoint because, the love of God has been poured out within our hearts through the Holy Spirit."*

God showed me in James 1:12 that we are blessed when we persevere under trial. When we are approved, He will give us a crown of life. He promises this because we love Him. It was clear that *life* refers not only to immortality and eternal life, but to glory and honor *now* in this life (see Romans 2:10, and John, 10:10).

I wanted to access this promise. So, what did God require of me? Micah 6:8 (NIV) states that I *"act justly and to love mercy and to walk humbly"* before my God. It is important also to remember steps one through four in the above paragraph.

The *evil* that caused our family's tribulation and distress was mainly *anger*. We thought if we just got angry enough that would fix Todd's problems! It was obvious we could not control Todd with all his complicated emotions by becoming irate.

Without the wisdom from God, we were fighting a losing battle. God is so faithful to teach and train us when we ask. We finally did ask God for wisdom.

In order to give up control, we had to acknowledge that we needed help. We had to trust God to rescue us from ourselves. We thought it was our job to *control* our children. We really didn't understand God meant for us to have faith in Him for everything in our lives, including raising our children. We wanted to be counted with the blessed of God. So, we wanted to continue to endure trials and test because, as

James 5:11 (NASB) says, *"Behold we count those blessed who endured."* No one has endured more than Job of the Old Testament, except for Jesus. I noticed the outcome of the Lord's dealing with Job. The story of Job tells of his unequaled loss of health, children, home, and everything except for his wife, who told him to curse God and die. Job, being unaware of Satan's intent, made the statement in Job 1:21 (NASB) that, *"the Lord gives and the Lord takes away."* God rebuked Job for his *"words without knowledge"* (Job 38:2, NASB).

God gives life. He does not take the lives of His people. We sometimes forget that, as James 5:11b (NASB) says, *"The Lord is full of compassion and is merciful."*

I notice that God always took the blame for all the bad things under the old law. I realized it was because *Jesus had not yet come to destroy*--some translations say *expose*-- *the works of the devil* (I John 3:8b, NASB).

John 14:8 showed me that when Jesus came, He also revealed *"Abba" Father* to us. Even though God appeared to be harsh to the Old Testament saints, I learned through obedience God walked beside them and He blessed them. The New Testament showed me the true nature of God the Father through Jesus and His sacrificial love for me and all mankind.

Jesus' sacrifice ushered in a new and better covenant with more and better promises. How exciting to know He now lives inside us by His Spirit. His indwelling

Presence gives me access to all His blessings. I am now under *grace*, and through faith in His Word, I'm able to discern both good and evil, which allows me to make a conscious choice. As I walk through life receiving His peace and joy in the midst of trials as *more* than a conqueror, He encourages me to bless, comfort, and help others.

I counted the phrase, *"God's mercy endures forever"* forty-three times in the Bible, from I and II Chronicles, Ezra, Psalms, and Jeremiah. It was interesting to me that even God had to practice *endurance* with His people. The Bible says to,

> *Run with endurance the race that lies before us, keeping our eyes on Jesus, the source and protector of our faith. Who for the joy that lay before Him, endured a cross and despised the*

More Years of Trial

shame, and has sat down at the right hand of God's throne. For consider Him who endured such hostility From sinners against Himself so that you won't grow weary and lose heart.

— Hebrews 12: 1b, 2-3, HCSB

Jesus *endured the cross* so I would not grow weary and lose heart while enduring the trials in my life. Wow! His love overwhelms me when I think about all He endured for me.

Caring, loving, heavenly Father,

Teach Larry and me to continue to persevere

when we cannot control the things that happen to us in life.

Help us to learn in our struggle against anger that Your discipline

will help us produce the fruit of love in our family.

Help Larry and me, Todd, Jill, and Trent become more like Jesus.

Thank You.

In Jesus name,
Amen

Chapter 11

Effectual Prayer

The Fervent Prayer of a Righteous Man is Powerful and Effective.

– James 5: 16b, NIV

It was such a revelation to Larry and me when we discovered effectual prayer meant praying with faith and not doubting. I didn't know how to pray fervent, believing prayers because we had always been taught that God would answer, "yes," "no," or "maybe later," but II Cor. 1:17-20 tells a different story. Refer to Chapter 5, and read the entire scripture reference.

We learned we could be confident that God would listen to us when what we asked was in line with His promised will, that we could find what God's will was by reading the Bible, His "Last Will and Testament."

I believe more people would pray if they realize it is just a way of talking to God and believe they will receive all that the Word of God promises. We read in the Bible how Jesus, through His death, made it possible for us to approach God's throne of grace and make it possible to receive Jesus as our Lord and Savior. John 14:6 says that Jesus is the *only way* to the Father.

Larry and I had received Jesus as our Lord and Savior,

but that didn't mean we knew what the Bible taught about how to pray effectively especially about raising a "special needs" child. We were about to learn!

Since Larry and I worked at the Children's Home in Ontario, California before we adopted Todd, we thought we knew everything about how to care for children. We managed eighteen boys from ages six to eighteen years of age no problem! Raising one child should have been a breeze, right? Wrong! God said there was still much to learn about raising children, so He gave us Todd.

Faithless or not, when family and friends prayed for us, especially for Todd, we were so encouraged. When my sister, Elaine, who was five years older than me, prayed with me on the phone, she would lift my spirits and leave me with a word of wisdom from the Lord.

Elaine was a very knowledgeable Bible student. She had studied Greek and Hebrew, and I learned a lot about praying effectively from her. Elaine encouraged and strengthened my faith. One time when I was lamenting over my lack of parenting and coping skills concerning Todd, she said, "Hey, don't be so hard on yourself. *God was the perfect parent and His kids rebelled!"* That did make me feel a whole lot better.

When Todd was about three, he got mad and out of control, shoving all the pegs off the pegboard because he couldn't fit the pegs in the board. He never tried again. This became a pattern whenever he was unable to accomplish anything physically that he wanted to do; he never tried to do that particular thing again.

At that young age, it would have been the perfect time to stop and say, "Honey, let's talk to God about this and see what He tells us to do." Instead, we'd get frustrated ourselves and try frantically to help him do whatever he was trying to do and that only made him feel more discouraged. We wanted so desperately for Todd to be able to do things physically. We were definitely in denial. Larry and I would not accept the fact that Todd had a serious problem, especially one that we couldn't fix!

Starting when he was just a child, we tried to make him do an activity. Sometimes it *was* successful, such as the time when he was just three years old, and we got him a tricycle that he was unable to ride. I had him sit on the tricycle; I placed his feet on my hands as if they were the peddles and had him push with his feet on my right hand then on my left hand, and he would do that without any difficulty. Then I put his feet on the peddles, but he wouldn't push on them. I was determined he would ride that tricycle, so I had him sit on it every day for fifteen minutes until one day he yelled, "Ma-Ma, I ride my bike!" It was good and exciting that I could praise him for being able to finally ride his tricycle.

When Todd began to display irritating mannerisms and a defiant attitude, and even though we were beginning to be aware that God promised His Holy Spirit as our guide and helper, we still reacted irrationally. We needed to calmly say, "Todd, let's ask God to help us."

Even though we didn't pray with Todd when he was out of control at an early age, there were times we did think to pray to calm him down when he was older. God was always faithful to help us calm him down. I have to say, as the kids do, "DUH!"

God, forgive us for the times we would get so angry that we didn't want to pray. When we were too angry to pray with Todd, we could have stopped, gone into another room, taken a deep breath, knelt down, and prayed by ourselves. In time, God would have softened our hearts and Todd's too. Then we could have prayed on the spot with him. It would also have been a good practice to engage in with Jill and Trent.

Had we known the power of praying in faith with no doubting when Todd was a little boy, this story would have been very different. If we had depended on our heavenly Father for help in every situation, by the time Todd approached his teens, he would have gotten to know God too as his Abba Father, healer, protector, provider, and *"an ever-present help in trouble"* (Psalms 46:1, NIV).

Parents are sure to encounter problems in raising any child. One reason I wanted to share our story is to help parents (also newlyweds that are looking forward to having a family) realize the wonderful gift we have in the person of the Holy Spirit. It would have been such a blessing to have understood *His ever-present help* before our children became young adults. However, better late than never. The Spirit was still there even many times when we were not aware of His intervention. But even better when we know to call upon Him in our times of need.

Larry served as a deacon where we attended church, and people presumed Todd would take a more active part in worship and other church activities. As a teenager, he was aware of the expectations from the people there and also from us.

There were unacceptable behaviors like smoking. He was also looked down on by some because of his conduct, like looking at the bottom of his shoe and coughing and other obsessive-compulsive tendencies.

The pressure proved to be more than he could bear, so he started attending the Abundant Life Church in town. He liked to go to that church because they accepted him as he was. This was a good Spirit-filled church that taught about believing prayer. I was proud of him for never leaving the Lord and finding a place he could worship. He learned a lot while attending there.

The Bible says in 1 Thess. 5:17 (KJV) to, *"Pray without ceasing."* That told me I can talk to God anywhere, anytime. Realizing that, He then became my constant friend and companion. I love talking to Him all during the day.

During the time when Todd went to jail, we wanted to encourage him in some way, so each of us wrote prayers to him. Todd brought these "prayer letters" home from jail with him. I saved them not knowing at the time why I saved them or that I would write this book, but God knew. That showed me one way He directs our path (see Prov. 3:5 & 6).

I have found God reveals His purpose and His master plan for my life at the exact time that I need to know, one step at a time. A perfect example is this book. Step by step is recorded in the Bible this way, where Isa. 28:10 (KJV) and II Cor. 3:18 (KJV) say, respectively, *"Line upon line"* and *from "glory to glory."* As I complete one task, God already has the next thing prepared for me to do. He has truly been my guide and taught me not to be anxious, as well as to trust Him to accomplish all He has planned for me to do. Knowing He has everything all worked out, I don't have to worry about what I am to do next.

Prayer always helped me control my emotions, I gained strength and encouragement. It became easier to trust God and rely on His faithfulness as we faced the challenges that lie ahead.

I will say drugs were involved in Todd spending some time in jail. He asked that I not go into detail about all the reasons he had to go to jail. The judge originally did not sentence Todd to jail as he did not think he deserved a jail sentence. Instead, he was to go through Teen Challenge. We took him to Bakersfield's Teen Challenge, and all would have been fine had he completed his time there. However, he and another boy decided to leave and go to Sacramento.

When he came home, he did not follow through with his probation. Consequently, he had a warrant out for his arrest and eventually he had to spend his time in jail.

Letters of Encouragement to Todd

I'm sharing the prayers of Jill and Trent with you; they revealed their hearts toward their big brother when he was in trouble. I also share another special letter. While I was writing this book, Todd re-read these prayers. He was very touched as he realized he was truly loved. The letters now meant more to him than when he received them the first time.

Jill's Prayer Letter (Age fifteen)

Dear Lord, first of all, thanks for giving me my older brother, Todd. Help Todd to see how much I love him and all, because sometimes I forget to tell him and show him. Because he means a lot to me, I'm praying that you will keep your hand on his life, so that no matter what happens, he'll feel your love. All things work together for good for those who love God and are called according to your purpose, and I know Todd loves You. Help this situation although it's hard; work together for good in the end like you promised.

I know Todd has something very special to do and help him to seek it and find it in his life.

Miraculously My Own

Help him to use this experience to his benefit and hear him when he's crying and hurting inside. Please Lord, keep Todd safe and give him insight to your work, so that he can recognize your help when it comes.

We all care for Todd but it's sometimes hard for Todd to accept love. I feel I don't deserve love either, so help both Todd and me to remember that you love us. No one deserves your love; it's a <u>free gift</u>. Please help us take that gift and hold it close.

"Nothing can separate us from the love of Christ." Help us take that love and be filled with it so we can give it to others, please be with Todd and help him in everything he does.

With all the meaning I have,
(Jill drew a heart here.)

In Christ name, Amen

Jill

P.S. Todd, I really do love you, and I'm praying for you. How can I forget my big brother??!! Love ya!!

Trent's Prayer Letter (Age thirteen)

Dear heavenly Father,

Be with Todd and all of us during these trying times. May any direction Todd takes, Your hand be on him. Thank You for Your Son who forgave us all. We thank You for keeping watch over us.

In Jesus Name, Amen

Trent

A Special Letter

March 14, 1983

To Todd,

"My dear son be strong in the grace that is in Christ Jesus. Endure hardship with us like a good soldier of Christ Jesus. If anyone competes as an athlete, he does not receive a victor's crown unless he competes <u>according to the rules!</u> The hard-working farmer should be the first to receive a share of the crops. Reflect on what I am saying for the Lord will give you insight into all this. That we might obtain the salvation that is in Him with eternal glory.

Here is a trustworthy saying: If we died with Him, we will also live with Him.

If we disown Him, He will also disown us.

If we are faithless, He will remain faithful,

Miraculously My Own

For He cannot disown Himself.

Remember, God does not want us to <u>quarrel about words</u>: it is not of value, and only ruins those who listen. Present yourself to God as one approved a workman who does not need to be ashamed and who correctly handles the Word of God. Avoid godless chatter, because those who indulge in it will become more and more ungodly. Their teaching will spread like gangrene. Nevertheless, God's solid foundation stands sealed with this inscription.

The Lord knows who are His, and everyone who confesses the name for the Lord <u>must turn away from wickedness!</u>

In a large house there are not only articles of gold and silver, but also of wood and clay, some are for noble purposes and some for ignoble. If a man cleanses himself from the later (ignoble), he will be an instrument for noble purpose made holy, useful to the Master and prepared to do any good work.

Flee the evil desires of youth, and pursue righteousness, faith, love and peace, along with those who call on the name of the Lord out of a pure heart. Don't have anything to do with foolish and stupid arguments, because you know they produce quarrels, instead you must be kind to everyone, able to teach not resentful.

It is my prayer that God will give you a change of heart leading you to knowledge of the truth, and you will <u>come to your senses</u> and escape from the trap of the devil who has taken you captive to do His will. "Grace, mercy, and peace from God the Father and Christ Jesus our Lord."

(Underline Emphasis Mine)

Your Father and Brother in Christ,

St. Paul the apostle,

Also, to Todd with love, from Dad and Mom.

Taken from II Timothy, Chapter 2. (NIV) Not a direct quote.

The Lord impressed on me that Paul was writing not only to Timothy, but to all young men, so we sent the Apostle Paul's letter to Todd also as a personal word from him.

Todd seemed appreciative to have received the letters, as tears welled up in his eyes. He is very tender-hearted. I had always loved that about him, though he tries not to show it.

I do not want to leave the impression that we only prayed with and for our children when they were frustrated and or in trouble. However, we could have spoken more encouraging words to them to build them up. We needed to emphasize their talents and abilities. We could have even prayed Psalms 91 over them daily. Just before school, summer camp, wherever they were going, even if they were staying home. The Psalm says that God will give His angels charge over us and that no evil will come near our household. What a great promise for us to cling to. I noticed that all God's promises have conditions. Psalm 91 (NASB) are:

1) Make the Most High your dwelling place. (Vs.1)
2) Say, "the Lord is my refuge and my fortress" (Vs.2)
3) Trust Him. (Vs. 2b)
4) Love Him and know His name. (Vs 14b)

I hear you say, "Oh, Joyce, you don't know my child. He/she wouldn't want me to pray with them." Maybe not at first; I thought that, too, but just kneel down and pray beside him/her. If you think it best, go into another room, kneel down, and pray by yourself. God's Word is true. Your child will begin to calm down and eventually want to pray with you. I found the problem was not with Todd. We were the ones who didn't want to pray when we would get angry and so out of control.

I know now it was God's love for Larry and me that we experienced these difficult years. He wanted us to grow and develop as parents and mature children of God. God allowed many things in our life to humble and help us become more disciplined. Some were negative and some were positive, depending on our ability to listen and receive. As we were able to hear the promptings of the Holy

Spirit, we began to gain victory over our circumstances and make better decisions concerning Todd's, and all the family's, needs.

Prayer and Fasting

While learning about guidance through prayer, I also discovered fasting helped me to hear from the Holy Spirit. Isa. 58 (NASB) tells us that, *"fasting loosens the bands of wickedness undoes heavy burdens, lets the oppressed go free, and breaks every yoke."* This chapter also says when we fast, *"health will spring forth speedily, and our righteousness shall go before us, and the glory of the Lord shall be our reward"* (Isaiah 58, NASB). What a marvelous promise and encouragement to fast!

Jesus fasted, it says in Matt. 4:2 (KJV), until *"He hungered"* (forty days). I fast every year and have for several years. However, one year I felt in my heart that the Lord called me to fast for forty days. I ate nothing, but I did drink water. After about three days, I was not hungry, but I learned through Jesus' example that when I did begin to *hunger,* I needed to eat. Everyone is different. God lets us know (through our body) when to stop fasting. If we don't stop, we will begin to do damage to our body.

I found the taste of water from different sources was amazing as some are salty tasting, some sweet, or some slightly bitter. I began to eat some soup about a week before the forty days were up because I did begin to feel hungry. After fasting that long, it would not have been good for me to eat anything heavy for several days.

I had just started this fast when Larry's mom had the stroke that I related in the previous chapter. It did complicate *my plan* to spend more quiet time with God. There are times God calls us to do something totally opposite of what is on our mind. I wanted to get off all by myself and meditate and pray and just spend quality time with the Lord. Just the same, my fast was very beneficial; I think it helped me more than I realized to get through that difficult year. In Isaiah's description above of the benefits of fasting, I would say I received the *"undoes heavy burdens"* (Isaiah 58, NASB). I felt the release from all the pressure of Mom's stroke and dealing with Todd's problems that had escalated at that time. I was sure that was why God called me to do that long a fast at that particular time.

Larry and I had seven and a half years with no children, time we could have devoted to prayer, fasting, meditation, praising, and getting closer to God. However, I think we thought we knew all that was necessary about God and spiritual matters. We did not know we could have a close, intimate relationship with our Savior and God.

The Lord was patient, and He loved us so much that He gave us Todd to help us in our disciplining process. God was able to guide our hearts to desire Him as our Savior *and Lord*. He had always been our Savior, but being our

Lord has been and still is a

Process. Larry and I are so grateful to know we can be confident in the guidance from the Holy Spirit. Through prayer and fasting, we are assured He will guide us in our decisions concerning Todd and our family.

We received a beautiful, thought-provoking writing from an email. It fit so well with the theme of my book, of needing *God's guidance* in regards to our children, I just had to print it for all to enjoy.

Dancing with God

> *"When I meditated on the word Guidance, I kept seeing "dance" at the end of the word. I remember reading that doing God's will is a lot like dancing. When two people try to lead, nothing feels right.*
>
> *The movement doesn't flow with the music. And everything is quite uncomfortable and jerky. When one person realizes that, and lets the other lead, both bodies flow with the music. One gives cues, perhaps with the nudge to the back or by pressing lightly in one direction or another. It's as if two become one body, moving beautifully. The dance takes surrender, willingness and attentiveness from one person and gentle guidance and skill from the other.*

Miraculously My Own

My eyes drew back to the word GUIDANCE, when I saw "G" I thought of God, followed by "U" and "I." "God," "U," and "I" dance." God, you, and I dance. As I lowered my head, I became willing to trust that I would get guidance about my life.

Once again, I became willing to let God lead.

My prayer for you today is that God's blessings and mercies be upon you on this day and every day. May you abide in God as God abides in you. Dance together with God, trusting God to lead and guide you through each season of your life.

Eline L. Guercio

Father, Help me to dance with you daily.
In Jesus name, Amen

Chapter 12

The Loving Act of Discipline

The Rod and Reproof Give Wisdom.

— Prov. 29:15, KJV

When we were disobedient, my earthly father would send my sister or me into the bathroom to spank us. He would say, "Go to the bathroom." Oh, how we hated to hear those words. His *"rod"* was a double razor strap (I wouldn't recommend that). I'm sure sending us to the bathroom gave Daddy time to cool off.

Neither of our parents ever embarrassed us in public. They would just quietly say, "You're in trouble when you get home." We would try to be so perfect until we got home. We hoped they would forget our inappropriate behavior. I thought they did forget sometimes, but now I'm sure they decided that making us worry about the punishment was enough. My father spanked hard, probably harder than necessary, but I was never afraid of him. I'm grateful my parents never slapped me or used their hands. I associate my dad's razor strap as the object of correction to discipline me, not my dad's hand.

Though Daddy was a strict disciplinarian, he balanced it by being a loving and caring father who sang and rocked me to sleep. I don't know how old I was, but I remember I got so big that my hand could touch the floor as he rocked. I can still hear his beautiful tenor voice as he sang to me. He also was a great storyteller and told my sister and me funny and sometimes scary stories.

Eph. 6:4 (NASB) says, *"Fathers do not provoke your children to anger; but bring them up in the discipline and instruction of the Lord."* I noticed that scripture is directed specifically to the father as the disciplinarian and teacher of the Word. However, if the father is absent or not following God's instructions, then the mother or caregiver has to be the one to obey God's directions for disciplining.

Larry and I found many of the problems our family experienced were related to our lack of Biblical discipline, especially toward Todd. We were much too harsh with Todd because we wanted him to be like other children and stop the obsessive compulsive and rebellious behaviors. It embarrassed us, and we thought it made *us* look like bad parents. That old pride cropped up again and again, as it did when he trashed the house and had to go to the hospital. We wanted everything that was going wrong in our family to go away and Todd to become "normal" before anyone found out. We thought it was our job to *make* that happen. Jill and Trent didn't receive much physical punishment, but we were unaware of their needs and therefore the harshness for them was in the form of emotional neglect.

The reason there is so much controversy when it comes

to spanking a child is because so many of us administer it irresponsibly. God gave specific instructions about spanking and why we should spank. The Spirit impressed on my heart that there are two times in particular that we needed to spank our children. When their actions would prove dangerous to them, and when they out-and-out defied us.

Many times, just calmly warning Todd about the use of "the rod" would be enough to solve the problem. However, constantly warning (threatening) Todd resulted in him not believing we were serious and caused resentment and/or a rebellious spirit.

Larry and I plead guilty that when Todd defied us and we were out of control and we would give him contracts, take away his heavy metal music, or spank him with a belt, he just became more rebellious and resentful. To avoid that kind of reaction, spanking needs to be applied with love, prayer, and concern, or resentment will build up in children.

When Todd was older and we tried to control his outburst, it would end up in a physical fight. I would get in between him and his father and try to stop them from fighting. If I couldn't stop them, then I'd call one of the kids to call the police. Threatening that I would call the police sometimes stopped them, as they were embarrassed to have the police come to our house in order to calm them down. When nothing *we tried* worked, we realized we needed spiritual guidance.

First of all, the kind of discipline a parent uses

depends upon how severely a child is handicapped. Some children are so severely handicapped that many parents shy from any kind of discipline, especially spanking, and spanking is *not* always appropriate. Having said that, I want to emphasize the importance of godly discipline for children like Todd who *can understand* why they are being disciplined.

God being a God of grace helped Larry and me to see we needed discipline that would help our children become good, upright citizens who would be polite, kind, and loving people. Therefore, He would encourage time outs, denying amusements, or anything that would avoid having to spank our children. Sadly, there are some children and some situations when spanking cannot be avoided.

The Word of God uses the expression *THE ROD* as the instrument to apply physical discipline. This said to me that I should use a certain object like a paddle, stick, switch, or belt, known to the child as The Rod of Correction. Prov.22:15 (KJV) says,

> *"Foolishness is bound up in the heart of a child; but The Rod of Correction shall drive it far from him." God emphasized the rod (something other than our hand) as the proper instrument of punishment. Our hands needed always to be an extension of our love.*

Another scripture to encourage us is:

The Loving Act of Discipline

It is for discipline that you endure; God deals with you as sons, for what son is there whom his father does not discipline? But if you are without discipline of which all have become partakers, then you are illegitimate children and not sons. Furthermore, we have earthly fathers to discipline us, and we respect them, shall we not much rather be subject to the Father of spirits and live?

For they discipline us for a short time as it seemed best to them, but He disciplines us for our good, that we may share His holiness. All discipline for the moment seems not to be joyful, but sorrowful; yet those who have been trained by it, afterwards, it yields the peaceful fruit of righteousness.

— Heb. 12:7-11, NASB

STOP - THINK – PRAY

Starting early in our children's life, less physical punishment would not have been necessary had we learned to do three things: 1) stop, 2) think, and 3) pray.

I found that Todd and other adopted and/or handicapped children could be the most demanding and could get worse as they get older. These children were children, and they disobeyed the same as other children. I had a friend with an autistic child, now a pre-teen, who attacked her mom, as well as hit and bit her. The mother had to literally take her down to control her as we had to do with Todd. I would not say this child was spoiled, but some adopted and handicapped children, like this girl and Todd, believe they have gotten cheated out of a normal life and carry a chip on their shoulder most of the time.

The Holy Spirit reveals things to us as we pray and meditate. We did not "stop, think, and pray" as our children were growing up. We hadn't taken the time, nor did we know we needed to meditate and spend personal time with the Lord.

The Bible lets us know in Eph. 6:12 (NASB) that, *"our struggle is not against flesh and blood* [people, Todd in particular, our fight was not with him] *but against the rulers, and against the powers, against the world forces of this darkness, against the spiritual forces of wickedness, in the heavenly places."*

We, as a society, have done our children a great disservice by neglecting this loving part of child rearing. Yes, I said loving.

In Prov. 13: 24 (NIV), it says, *"He that spares the rod hates his son, but he who loves him is careful to discipline him."* Prov. 23: 13, 14 (NIV) warns us, *"Do not withhold discipline from a child; if you punish him with the rod, he will not die. Punish him with the rod and save his soul from death."*

Now that we were open and ready to listen to the Holy Spirit's guidance, we could apply the above three principles. Our children were almost grown by the time we began to listen. How great it might have been to have known when our children were young how to listen to the Spirit's instructions on raising them.

Maybe you are saying, "Well, what *are* those instructions?" The Holy Spirit is no respecter of persons. He will give you specific instructions for each child's individual need. Every child is different, and God is the only one who knows their exact need. His Spirit will instruct you so you will provide proper guidance for the disciplining and developing of their whole being (spirit, soul, and body). Prov. 22:6a (AMP) says, *"Train up a child in the way he should go, [and in keeping with his individual gift or bent] and when he is old, he will not depart from it."*

There has been progress in our family so it is never too late as you will see at the end of our story.

Father in heaven,

I Praise You and thank You God that when we pray, You are there to guide us in all areas of our lives.

Especially, teaching us that discipline is a loving act that You do for our benefit. In the same manner and purpose, help Larry and me discipline our children.

In Jesus Name, Amen

Chapter 13

Why Praise?

I will call upon the Lord, Who is worthy to be praised: so, shall I be saved from my enemies.

— Psalms, 18:3, KJV

I thought I had written all the chapters I was to write in this book when God spoke to my heart that I needed to write a chapter on praise. Why it is an important spiritual weapon of warfare, and why is it parents need to know this outflow of God's power?

Webster's New World Dictionary tells us praise comes from the Latin word "price." When we praise something, we are saying that we put a very high price on it.

Unger's Bible Dictionary says in Heb. 13:15-16, praise is metaphorically represented as a "sacrificial offering."

Larry and I discovered the real power of praise is when we offer it up to God while sick or depressed, praising and exalting Him in word and/or song. Praising Him when it is the last thing we want or feel like doing shows a grateful heart in place of a doubtful heart full of fear and complaints.

On Christmas Eve a couple of years ago, I experienced this power myself. Our daughter Jill and family from Simi

Valley were staying the night. I started having the most terrible pain all down the left side of my body, from my shoulder all down my ribcage, and all the way down to my hip. I had never felt such pain. Everyone had gone to bed ready for Santa to come in the morning. I just couldn't wake anyone up, on *that* night, to take me to the hospital for an emergency! I began praying, and then I remembered the stories in the Bible about praise and that God inhabits our praise, so I began to sing praises, just making up the words to my Father in heaven. Though singing certainly was the last thing I felt like doing--I really felt like crying.

    I determined to just think of all the wonderful things God had done in my life and continued to praise Him. The pain began to ease up as soon as I began to sing praises, and I praised Him until I was completely free of all pain! I'm not sure how long that was but I would estimate at least an hour.

    I went to the doctor on the following Monday to see if there was anything I needed to know that could have caused the pain, but my x-rays were fine and all test were negative. I was totally healed! Yes! Praise God!

    I am learning to completely trust God no matter how bad I feel or how difficult my situation may be. I want to love Him and know He will never leave me or forsake me. Abba Father says in His Word that He desires to give me all things to enjoy when I truly love and trust Him. However, I cannot use Him like a magical genie. Neither

Why Praise?

can I manipulate Him by using a man-concocted formula to get something I might want or need. When my praise is real and from the heart, God is touched, and because of that trust and faith, He rewards me openly and freely. I Tim. 6:17 (NASB) says that He, *"richly supplies us with all things to enjoy."*

I love praising God in word and in song. Spending time praising and blessing the
Lord is another way we learned to hear the voice of the Spirit, to guide, comfort, and direct us. We receive God's enlightenment through the heart felt praise and adoration of Him (Father, Son and Holy Spirit).

Psalms 134:2 (KJV) tells us to, *"Lift up our hands in the Sanctuary and Bless the Lord."* In I Tim. 2:8 (NASB), God tells us He wants, *"Men in every place to pray, lifting up holy hands without wrath and dissension."*

When praise is sacrificial it reflects a repentant, humble heart. In Psalms 67:3, praise is translated as "Hands to God" in Hebrew. When Larry and I raise our hands, it demonstrates an outward expression of our inward devotion, dependence, and an act of submission. It also testifies that we completely trust God with our daily struggles and battles. Lifting up our hands in praise not only shows we depend on God, but also acknowledges He is our true source for every need.

We found that praise stopped the Devil in his tracks, but he could not be our focus. Our thoughts had to be on glorifying God with a loving and devoted heart.

I'm convinced the best time to praise is when we begin our day. It is like "tithing" our time and "offering" our praise in the morning. I here confess my own neglect and lack of discipline. The times I do start my day praising God, giving Him the first of my day, things go well, and I accomplish so much more. I'm an evening person, and I have a hard time getting up early, especially when the devil manages to manipulate my thoughts, with ideas like, "I'm so tired," "it's too cold," "I didn't get much sleep last night," etc.

I'm not intending praise to be a legalistic ritual that we must do. I just know blessings and benefits come from submitting to God, especially when we obey His command. Deut. 6: 5 (NIV) says, *"Love the Lord your God with all your heart and with all your soul and with your strength."*

I know when I start my day praising and loving the Lord, it prepares my mind and heart and brings me into a closer relationship with Him so I can make better decisions during the day.

I know I need to give God the first fruits (tithing the gross) of our income. Giving Him the first fruits of my time (day) is no different. When I honor God in this way, He honors me and my family with guidance, protection, favor and wisdom throughout our day. To help me rise early in the morning, I am trying to put the following into practice. It might be helpful for others to consider:

Why Praise?

1) Go to bed earlier, though I am a night person, for all things are possible with God. He also promises to give His beloved sleep.

2) Arrange my schedule to allow more time to seek the Lord.

3) Pray for the Holy Spirit to wake me early (He has done this many times).

4) Ask the Holy Spirit to guide me as to what I need to do to accomplish an effective early morning praise and worship.

5) Most important, *never give up.* When I fail, I 'm determined to just start again, then one day I know morning praise and worship will become a normal part of my day.

I found a good example of the power of praise in I Chronicles 23:30. David, a biblical warrior of God, instructed the priests to stand every morning to "thank and praise the Lord and do the same in the evening" (I Chronicles 23:30, NIV). I Peter 2:5-9 (ESV) informed me that we are now "A chosen race a royal priesthood" in the kingdom of our Lord. What an amazing revelation!

When Jehoshaphat went to war in the Old Testament, and (Vs.21) after consulting the people he had men to sing to the Lord and to praise the Lord for the splendor of His holiness, as they went out ahead of the army, saying, "Give thanks to the Lord; for His love endures forever". (Vs. 22) "As they began to sing and praise, the Lord set ambushes against the men of Ammon and Moab and Mount Seir who were invading Judah, and they were defeated" (Vs 27) [Then they] returned joyfully to Jerusalem, for the Lord had given them cause to rejoice over their enemies. (Vs 29-30) The fear of the Lord came upon all the kingdoms of the countries when they heard how the Lord had fought against the enemies of Israel. And the kingdom of Jehoshaphat was at peace, for his God had given him rest on every side.

— II Chronicles 20:21-30, NIV

Another example is in II Kings 3:15 (NIV), when Elisha said to the king of Israel, *"'bring me a harpist.' While the harpist was playing, the hand of the Lord came upon Elisha. Then, God did many miraculous things and Israel defeated the Moabite army."*

God will fight our battles for us if we start our day with praise, prayer, and reading His Word; it is also the best way to protect our family from the devil's onslaughts, especially when we do not feel like praising.

What does all this have to do with our son Todd? First of all, giving praise to God would have given our home the uplift and joy it truly needed. Rather than trusting God and praising Him for all He was doing in our lives, we felt depressed and defeated, thereby, opening the door for the devil to work in our family. How great to have been aware of the power of praise when we were raising our children, especially Todd.

Why Praise?

The Holy Spirit would have guided us so we would have been sensitive to what was going on (insights into Todd, Jill, and Trent's emotional needs) and prevented many problems that were mounting as our family grew. How great to be forewarned of problems *before* someone in our family was traumatized! Praise is truly preventive medicine because in Psalms 22:3, God tells us He inhabits our praises.

We eventually receive God's enlightenment through the heart felt praise and adoration of Him (Father, Son and Holy Spirit). Praise enabled us to hear what the Spirit said to do in order to win the battles we were facing and still do. One thing He revealed to us was that in our effort to meet Todd's special needs, we had been neglecting the emotional needs of our other children.

When Todd was an infant, we were so concerned that he wouldn't grow up healthy and whole. It became such a habit to concentrate on all his difficulties that by the time Jill (three-and-a-half years later) and Trent (five years later) came along, we didn't realize we were still focusing on Todd's needs. Subsequently, we neglected Jill and Trent's emotional needs.

Now that Jill and Trent are grown, they have made us aware that we sacrificed them in many ways in order to try to meet Todd's needs, like taking him to the psychologist once a week, sixth through eighth grade, while they waited. Jill and Trent had to go with me to look for Todd when he would take off from school or from our car when we were some places like the store, or when he took off from home. I constantly concentrated on Todd and his problems.

This was a very hard revelation for Larry and me to accept. They explained how hard it was for them to deal with the violence and chaos going on in the family.

My younger son, Trent, told me he went to Christian counseling. It helped him to understand why he was having so many problems in life. Most were from the frustrations of his childhood.

Our daughter believes she has forgiven us for the constant attention given to Todd's needs. That she has forgiven Todd for the trauma caused by his angry outbursts. However, she has to admit that every once in a while, those old feelings erupt, and she is still having to dig into the root of bitterness in order to free her heart from feelings of anger and resentment.

Once we started catering to Todd's "special needs," the problem only got worse. He started expecting it. Todd would become insulted and/or angry if he didn't get his way. Like Todd, many special needs children develop the same attitude; in other words, they can become selfish and spoiled. We are still struggling with this problem, though Todd is now a man. However, as the years go by, he is becoming more loving, appreciative, and thoughtful; I realize God is not finished with him or any of us yet.

I have noticed parents with special needs children often

Why Praise?

have the same problem. Parents get so involved with the "special needs child" that their other children's needs get ignored or minimized. It is hard to see this in ourselves. In my mind, I believed Jill and Trent could see the struggle we were having, and that they were strong enough to handle those situations. They could not! Children are children; they do not and cannot be expected to understand what is going on. Jill and Trent's needs were just as real to them and as needful as Todd's.

I do not have an answer of how not to enable your "special needs child." For one thing, every child is different. I do know that the Holy Spirit *is willing and able* to guide you if you will ask, believe, and do what He tells you to. I know praying and praising God and listening for His direction would have kept us from neglecting the needs of Jill and Trent and enabling Todd.

How I wish we had known the power of praise when our children started showing these warning signs:

1) A sudden drop in grades

2) Getting in fights

3) A change in personality (More hostile and irritable and/or uncommunicative)

4) Trying to be so perfect (which resulted in the tendency to be sneaky)

These signs show trouble brewing in a family. At times like this, through the power of prayer and praise, God may direct a family to go to Christian counseling. God provided the perfect example of the power of praise as a confirmation that I needed.

I was watching the *700 Club* on TV. An infant was born with Leukemia and was at the point of death. The doctors at the hospital sent the baby home to die as there was nothing they could do, and his breathing was labored. The mother started singing, "Open the

Eyes of My Heart Lord." Instead of dying, the baby started getting better. In the morning, they took him back to the hospital to have him checked. There was *NO SIGN OF LEUKEMIA!!!* Even the doctors said it was a real miracle. If you want to know the whole story of this baby, it aired on TV *700 Club* 2/22/07. I'm sure they will make it available to you.

Committing our life to Jesus and asking Him into our hearts, were the first steps to all God's blessings. If that is lacking in your life, please do it now. When we asked Jesus to baptize us with the Holy Spirit, that made it possible for us to take advantage of all the blessings He provided by his life, death, and resurrection. Next, we found a good, full gospel church.

Another important step Larry and I had taken many years ago was to repent and be baptized in water in order to have "a good conscience toward God" (I Peter 3: 21, NIV). Acts 2:38 (NIV) says it is, *"for the forgiveness of our sins."* Then we are also promised *"the gift of the Holy Spirit.*

The Holy Spirit guides us to all truth and protects our

Why Praise?

family from the enemy of our souls. We are learning to praise and pray more effectively, and I know in time, as James 5:16 says, that we will *accomplish much*. Isn't God wonderful and amazing to use praise as a weapon? We can just be joyful and thwart all the enemy's evil plans. Hallelujah!

Psalm of Praise

"Praise the Lord! Praise the Lord in His sanctuary;
Praise Him in His mighty expanse.
Praise Him for His mighty deeds;
Praise Him according to His excellent greatness.
Praise Him with trumpet sound;
Praise Him with harp and lyre.
Praise Him with timbral and dancing;
Praise Him with stringed instruments and pipe.
Praise Him with loud cymbals;
Praise Him with resounding cymbals.
Let everything that has breath praise the Lord.
Praise the Lord."

— Psalms 150, NASB

Miraculously My Own

Dear Father in heaven,

I thank You for showing us how to love You and tap into Your power, through the avenue of praise.

In Jesus name,

Amen

Chapter 14

Growing in My Faith

What Matters is Faith Working through Love.

— Gal. 5: 6, HCSB

My understanding of the word faith was for many years believing that God and Jesus existed, and that the Bible was the Word of God. All true; however, faith is much more than that. I needed to learn about the *force of faith* especially in order to be a godly parent.

What is Faith? Heb. 11:1 (KJV) tells us, "Now faith is the substance of things hoped for the evidence of things not seen."

I was curious to know the American College Dictionary's definition of *substance* and *evidence.* Substance is defined as physical matter or the material of which something is made. *Evidence* is defined as grounds for belief, proof, an indication or sign. I found it very fascinating that the dictionary defined faith as both tangible and proven belief, which agrees with the biblical definition.

When I received Jesus as my Lord and Savior and was baptized in water for the remission of my sins at the early age of nine, I believed that Jesus died, was buried, and rose again from the dead. I was baptized in the name of the

Father, Son, and Holy Spirit.

Nothing was ever mentioned about receiving the "gift" of the Holy Spirit, or being "filled" with the Spirit.

As expressed in Eph. 5: 18 (NIV), *"Do not get drunk on wine, which leads to debauchery. Instead, be filled with the Spirit."*

How? Luke 11:13 says to ask. My friend Joyce Megas gave me cassette tapes to listen to when I was going through the most difficult time with Todd. The tapes gave me scriptures to study on faith and the Holy Spirit and how I needed His power to be able to deal with all the complexities of life. At the time, my complexities were dealing with menopause, Todd, a teen and his problems, two other teens, keeping up with all their sport activities, and trying to do daily household chores, not to mention trying to be a good wife to Larry. I was pretty much a basket case.

I was taught my body was the temple of the Holy Spirit, though I didn't comprehend what that meant. I was not tempted to drink, smoke, or do drugs, as some of my friends were. I did not attribute that to the Spirit guarding me from the desire to sin, until many years later. Gal. 5: 24 (NASB) tells us, *"Now those who belong to Christ Jesus have crucified the flesh with its passions and desires."*

However, though I was not aware of His protection, He did protect me, especially when I was a vulnerable teenager and my earthly father had died. I will share this story as one

Growing in My Faith

example of God's protection through the guardianship of the Holy Spirit.

Two of my junior high girlfriends and I went to a movie in Fullerton. We lived in Buena Park, five miles away. I thought one of the girl's moms were to pick us up afterwards, but my friends had cooked up a scheme to walk home at night by ourselves! Each girl told their moms that the other mom was picking us up. They had not told me because they knew I wouldn't go along with that idea.

When I asked whose mom was picking us up, my friends started giggling and said we were going to walk home! So, we started walking home, and some college boys came along and offered us a ride. I said, "No," but my girlfriends thought it would be "fun."

We did go with them, though this could have been a very dangerous decision; the boys were very nice and did take us home. I know now that God prearranged the timing for those boys to come along. Realizing we were being foolish little girls, they decided they should protect us and take us home.

I became aware of how important it is to work toward replacing sin with the fruit of the Spirit, otherwise the tendency to sin became more alluring. I thank God for His forgiveness and grace as these fruits are not manifested perfectly in my life or ever will be, but they are my goal. Belonging to Christ keeps me pure only because of His marvelous grace through His blood that covers my sin as I repent. I'll continue to strive for perfection until Jesus comes because I know His grace will make up the difference.

Discovering the force of faith was the beginning of our finding a peaceful solution to our families' problems. Larry and I found understanding the deeper meanings of faith to be of number one importance.

The tremendous force of faith is truly miraculous. The book of Genesis says that God spoke the universe into existence by the power of faith when He said in Genesis 1:3 (NIV), "Let there be light and there was light!"

I was astonished to learn that God used the force of faith to create the world. God spoke, and the force of His faith created what He spoke. Our words, when spoken in faith, also have creative power. Proverbs 18:21 (KJV) says, "Death and Life are in the power of the tongue." It's as if light bursts forth from the people who came to Jesus for healing when Jesus told them, "Your faith has made you whole." That same force of faith is available to us today. I find that so wonderfully amazing! Romans 12:3 says:

"God has dealt to every man, the measure of faith" (KJV).

Since God gave Larry and me this measure of faith, and as we are learning to love God, He says He will give us power through His Spirit to accomplish anything. That would include managing a peaceful home. In Matt. 19: 26 (KJV), it says, "With God all things are possible."

I'm learning to hope for great things to glorify God in my life and in the lives of my children. One of those great things I hope for and believe is that God will use this book to help many families look to the Spirit for answers to all their needs.

MONEY: A LOVE BUSTER

One of the "fiery darts" Satan tried to destroy our family with was money!

Faith is a shield against those fiery darts. Gal. 5: 6 reminds us of that. Faith works by love. Satan messing with our finances caused much friction between Larry and me. Satan does this to many couples, causing some families to even break apart. He uses many things to distract people such as computers, TV, magazines, billboards, and movies. Also, he pressured us to keep up with our neighbors and friends.

Money was a constant concern; because of the damage to our home from Todd's outbursts of anger, there was damage to walls, and doors, etc. which had to be replaced. Todd's fight with O.C.D. was also a problem. We often needed new faucets from his pumping and turning them on and off, and the walls in the bathroom got mildew because his showers took an hour-long or lengthier. In addition, there was therapy and doctor appointments. We had insurance, but it never paid everything that was required for his special needs, and this caused so much tension and stress that we needed guidance from the Spirit in order for Larry and me to remain stable. Most of Todd's life, we weren't aware of the Spirit, so we were very unstable.

The subject of money can be very important to couples that have children with special needs. It can be a major problem for them as it was for us. Many times, these children need physical and/or mental therapy and in-home care of some kind.

GOD AND MONEY

> *"Now He who supplies seed to the sower and bread for food, will supply and multiply our seed for sowing and increase the harvest of our righteousness. You will be enriched in everything for all liberality, which through us is producing thanksgiving to God".*
>
> — II Cor. 9:10 & 11, NASB

Jesus says, in Matt. 6:24 (NIV), *"No one can serve two Masters. Either he will hate the one and love the other, or he will be devoted to the one and despise the other. You cannot serve both God and money."* I Tim. 6: 10 (NASB) says, *"The love of money is the root of all sorts of evil, and some by longing for it have wandered away from the faith, and pierced themselves with many a pang."*

I noticed God does not say money is evil but the ***love*** of money.

It didn't matter how organized or how money-wise we believed we were, we still needed to make it a priority to take a course in Financial Planning.

Christian financial planning gave us God's way of finance, and of course, His way is perfect. There are many good Christian financial planning groups or seminars to attend. It is never too late. Larry and I attended our first seminar, and we just had our fiftieth wedding anniversary. We can testify of its importance and value. The seminar helped our communication in this area and our determination to do a better job of being accountable for the money we spend. We are learning to work together and expect God's blessing when we follow His guidance, so we can then be a blessing to others. We will not get discouraged if we fail, we will just start again.

If we had started when we were young parents, we'd have had more time and money to build a savings. There would have been many more years for God to bless us and for us to be a blessing to others.

In Prov. 16: 9 (NIV) it says, *"In his heart a man plans his course, but the Lord determines his steps."* That tells me we must have a plan in order for God to guide us. God loves to take our plans and direct our steps to the right people at the right time in order to bless everyone involved.

Ultimately, He guides our steps toward His master plan.

I tried many years to work with Larry who handled the money, but he was not willing to work with me. Some people, like Larry, want total control of the money, and others do not want anything to do with the finances. Don't be discouraged. Continue to pray. God will get help your spouse to have a desire to work with you.

Larry and I are now making decisions together, but I wish it had not taken so many years. I'm grateful we never gave up. When we finally agreed to work together, I asked God to help me not to be resentful for all the years that we were unable to communicate about finances. I had to have a forgiving heart and be thankful now to be working as a team.

We didn't let Satan discourage us and tell us that we were never going to get out of debt. He is a liar. God always makes a way when there seems to be no way as that is how our Father in heaven is glorified.

For us to receive God's provision, we needed to repent and confess our lack of faith and discipline. Then ask Him to forgive us for not being good stewards of the money He provided for us. We knew all our money was really God's and how generous He was to only ask for a ten percent tithe. However, He also asked us to bring our offerings to His storehouse (Malachi 3:8). I believe that is where we received His greatest blessings.

In Phil. 4:6 and Mark 11:24, I found in order for us to

receive His promises we must plan to succeed. Then give thanks to God *before* we receive anything showing we believe and trust Him for the outcome.

The result will be II Cor. 9: 8, that God will *supply all our needs* and we will have an abundance to give to whatever need there is that comes our way.

Gal. 5:6 (NASB) says *faith works through love,* however, if money can be a "Love Buster" and our love became weak, what would have happened to our faith, since *faith works through love?* We did not let our financial situation weaken our love for one another, which in turn strengthened our faith. Faith, working by or through love, helped in bringing a peaceful solution to our family's difficult problems.

When doubt started to creep in, I would remember the little carved out and painted board my daughter Jill made for our twenty-fourth anniversary that said, "LOVE NEVER FAILS." I was then encouraged, and my faith became stronger to believe and not doubt.

My desire for peace for Todd, peace for Jill, peace for Trent, and peace for Larry and me, made me want to develop the powerful *force of faith* in and for my life. The solution and our assignment was to love God and one another more and more each day.

Miraculously My Own

Father,

Please help us to always abide in Your love, And then we can know we can speak words of faith and the force of faith will bring those words to pass.

As our faith becomes stronger, we will have the "peace that passes all understanding."

Thank You,

In Jesus' name,
Amen

Chapter 15

Abiding in God's Love

(The "Perfect Peace" Puzzle)

> *Just as the Father has loved Me, I have loved you. Abide in My love.*
>
> —John 15: 9, NASB

Larry and I knew the promises that said, *"Ask and it shall be given you."*

Matt. 7: 7 and John 15: 7 (NASB) says, *"If you abide in me and I abide in you ask whatsoever you wish, and it shall be done for you."* I had to find out *why* we were not receiving those promises of peace we so desperately needed.

During this very difficult time of dealing with Todd's eruptions, we needed a peaceful solution to the chaos going on in our home. I knew it wasn't God's fault.

Though I have studied God's Word most all my life, I used to have such a hard time concentrating on it. Then, when I began to think of it as God giving me this huge picture puzzle to fit together in order to see His perfect plan for my life, I really began to enjoy studying the Bible. When I would get all the pieces put together on any one subject, the picture (truth) would become crystal clear.

Miraculously My Own

If you knew me, you would understand why I compared the study of God's Word to working a jigsaw puzzle. For several years now, I have put together many 500-1000 piece puzzles a year. I have been studying God's Word most every day, so I guess you could say I have become more addicted to God's "Perfect Peace Puzzle," because I was determined to search and find the missing pieces in our family's "peace puzzle."

Even if you are not a big puzzle addict like me, this may be a way for you to make Bible study exciting and fun. Comparing Bible truths to puzzle pieces made studying the Word of God exciting and helped me to *rightly divide the Word of truth* (II Tim. 2:15, (NKJV).

In order to develop the peaceful fruit of the Spirit, I needed to find those pieces that would fit our family together. Through our experiences with Todd, God put the desire in my heart to write this story. He also put a deep yearning in me to help parents put their family's "picture puzzle" together.

The most important piece of the puzzle our family needed was the *"fruit of love"* piece. Not just the love piece, which I found in I Cor.13 (the love chapter in the Bible), but alongside it would have to be the *"Abiding in Love"* piece. I knew I had to find those pieces to receive the peace our family was seeking. I needed to receive the answer to the question, "How was it possible to *abide* in love?" God helped me find nine puzzle pieces (truths) as we sought to help Todd, answer the above question, and calm the storm raging in all of us.

(I Corinthians 13) Fruit of Love Piece

We had to learn to love unconditionally. Look at one another in love and acceptance. Realizing we can hate what a person is doing, but not the person.

(John 15:7) His Word Abiding in Us Piece

If we wanted to receive anything from the Lord, we had to know His Word in order for it to abide in us. This piece was necessary in order to even find the following pieces.

(John 15:10) Abide in Jesus' Love Piece

We needed to also abide in Jesus. Our ability to survive depended upon our receiving the spiritual nourishment from our Lord Jesus.

(Matthew 23:37-39) Keep My Commandments Piece

The answer to how we can abide in Jesus' love is to just keep His commandments. The most important one is to love the Lord our God with all our soul, mind, and strength, and to love one another just like Jesus loves us.

(John 15:1) Jesus, the Vine Piece

If we wanted to bear fruit for the Lord, we had to remain in Jesus. Apart from Him, we could not do anything.

(John 15:1) Abba Father, the Vinedresser (Gardener) Piece

The parts of us that were not bearing fruit (unused talents and abilities) the Father (vinedresser) would take away. But what we do use for the Lord will bear fruit, and the Father trims that fruitful part clean, the talents we are using to glorify the Lord, so we will become even more fruitful.

(John 15:3) The Branches (People) Piece

We certainly did not want to be cut off from Jesus. He said in verse three that as we abide in His Word, we are clean because of the words He spoke to us.

(John 15:11) The Joy of Jesus Piece

Jesus spoke these words so our family could learn about the joy of Jesus, because of all the struggles, our family certainly needed that joy.

(John 15:11b) Fullness of Joy Piece.

Best of all, Jesus wanted our joy to be full or complete. What a great goal to strive for, the fullness of joy.

I now had all the pieces to my Bible jigsaw puzzle, but the picture still didn't make any sense. Yes, the pieces to the "peace puzzle" were there to receive the peace we so desired, but now the hard part was we had to put them all together. In other words, we had to apply those truths to our lives.

I knew I had to have wisdom to be able to put into practice all these spiritual pieces. God promised to give us wisdom when we asked, and that He would give it liberally. What a great promise.

We not only heard *what* to do but now we had to *do*, as James 1:22 (HCSB) instructed us to do: *"Be doers of the word not hearers only, deceiving yourselves."* Doing what it says was our real challenge. When we were given God's wisdom to find the pieces, then we had to do what wisdom instructed. Otherwise, it would be like having all the pieces to a jigsaw puzzle and expect them to just fall in place or try to force them together the way we think they should fit.

If we did that, we would never get to see the beautiful picture or the wonderful plan God has for our life.

Larry and I started learning to love one another as the Bible says: being patient and kind to one another. We learned to abide in Jesus's love as we devoted time in prayer and meditation. Listening to the Spirit, we were able to apply those "attributes of wisdom," and the pieces began to fall into place as the picture of our family receiving Jesus' peace started to come into view.

I know we will never get all the pieces together *perfectly,* so what will make a complete picture? Our God's marvelous grace (unmerited favor) finishes what we cannot accomplish on our own. Praise God for continuing to help as we strive to finish our "Perfect Peace Puzzle!"

> *Our most gracious Father in heaven,*
> *Help Larry and me keep our mind on You and Your Word.*
> *Make Your love for us, our love for each other,*
> *and our love for You visible to our children*
> *so that all our family will be able to receive Your "Perfect Peace."*
> *Thank You,*
>
> *In Jesus name,*
> *Amen.*

Chapter 16

Todd's Own Story

He chose us in Him before the Foundations of the World, That, we should be Holy and Blameless before Him in Love.

— Ephesians 1: 4, NASB

When my mom first asked me to share the story of my life, I didn't really want to tell people my life story. I told Mom I wanted to forget the past. Mom then asked me if I thought it would help some young people and their parents, and if I would want to do that. I decided I would.

Mom said she believed this book to be God's plan and purpose for our lives. If that is true, God will see that many people will benefit from our experiences. I would like for that to happen, so I will try to believe that, too.

My Early Childhood Memories

When I was three, we had a dog named Tavish; actually, his name was McTavish. He was a wirehaired terrier. One day, I was sitting on the porch next to him, and I decided it would be fun to bite his ear, so I did! He yelped; he didn't think it was fun, so he bit me back, and I never did that again.

In pre-school, I had a wonderful and fun teacher; her name was Miss Mary. Miss Mary had a terrible accident, a head-on collision in her car. She was badly injured. It left her spastic. One would think she had been born with cerebral palsy. It was very sad. I loved Miss Mary and continued to visit her with my family for several years. When I started playing the accordion, I would play for her when we visited her, and it seemed to please her. I also played my accordion for my mom's friend's grandmother, who was in a rest home. I liked to play my accordion for people.

I was four when my little brother was born. I remember helping my parents name him. They gave me two names: Darrel and Trent. I liked the name Trent because it started with the letter "T" like my name. So that's what they named him.

I loved kindergarten, and I loved my teacher. At Easter, we were to draw something to do with Easter. I painted a picture of Easter eggs raining down from the sky and the Easter Bunny carrying an Easter basket full of eggs. My mom liked it so much, she framed it and hung it in the toy room, where it is still hanging today.

We went to visit my Aunt Elaine and Uncle Joe who lived in Louisiana when the astronauts first landed on the moon. I was five and so excited about the capsule return; I just had to draw the capsule floating down by parachute into

Todd's Own Story

the ocean. My aunt was amazed I could draw so well that she had me bring it with us to the children's T.V. program *Buckskin Bill*, and he showed them on T.V. that day.

***

At church there was a little old man who passed out candy to all the kids every Sunday. Everyone called him, "The Candy Man." My mom reminded me that he always warned the kids not to leave the candy wrappers anywhere inside or outside the church because, he said, they all had his name on them.

In second grade, I painted a picture of a red race car with black smoke coming out of the exhaust and a silhouette of a man driving. The teacher said it was really good and put it up on the display board. Another memory I have is when I was eight. Dad and Mom took us kids to the Japanese Deer Park, in Buena Park, California. At the deer park, they had a karate show. When we got home, my sister and I were trying to copy the karate performers. I was pretending to step on Jill, and Trent, who was three at the time, thought I was actually hurting Jill. He picked up a big rock to throw it at me, but it was so heavy he dropped it right on Jill's head. The rock was so big and heavy that Mom and Dad had to take Jill to the doctor for stitches. My sister knew Trent hadn't meant to hurt her.

My dad and I belonged to Indian Guides. We were the Black Foot tribe. Indian Guides are kind of like scouts; you do crafts, camp out, and earn badges. One time we camped out at Joshua Tree. We climbed on the big rocks and had a great time. I made my mom a necklace one time from paper clips.

When I was ten, we moved to Yucaipa from Fullerton. I was sad to leave my friends, Tim and Scott, and my school and friends there. I did come to like country life in Yucaipa. I liked our house, and I liked helping Dad in the yard. The yard was big and there were acres of fields around for us to explore. One field had a big tree; Jill, Trent, and I found a skeleton of a cat under it. We used to pretend the tree was a fort. At the bottom of our hill was another fenced in field with cattle, and we would go over the fence and sometimes the bull would chase us out.

The best things I thought about our country life were all the creatures like snakes, tarantulas, and other interesting things like frogs, scorpions, millipedes, and centipedes. All these things creeped my mom out, especially when I would catch a king snake and wrap it around my neck, knock on the window and show her. One time I found a tarantula; I picked it up and let it crawl on my arm. Mom looked out the window and saw me. She came out and said, "Todd, that spider could bite you!"

I told her I had read a book all about tarantulas, and it said they won't bite you unless you pinch their body. So, she let me play with it. We tried to keep one in a cage one time, but it wouldn't eat even though I caught grasshoppers to feed it (their favorite food), and then it died.

I was ten when I started school in Yucaipa. I was excited that the boys in my class said they were so happy to have another guy on their ball team. Because I was slow physically, they got mad at me. I felt so bad, I wanted to play ball with them, but they thought I was purposely not trying. That was the beginning of the teasing and tormenting I endured every day I went to school.

Starting junior high was exciting. I felt really grown up when I got my own locker with a combination lock. I also liked the idea of dressing out for P.E. and playing flag football. The kids continued to tease and daily torment me. They didn't understand my disability. One day, they made me eat flies, and then they called me, "fly eater."

While at that middle school a kid told me about marijuana and how it made him feel like walking on air. I was really curious but didn't try it then.

Wildwood School

Junior high through high school were very traumatic years for me, as well as my 20s and part of my 30s. Wildwood School had kids from the boy's home. They were kids who had been in trouble with the law. It also had kids who were different in some way. I was one of those kids. I hadn't been in trouble with the law at that point in my life. This part of my life story is hard for me to talk about. I want to share these difficult years in hopes it will prevent some kids from making the same mistakes I made.

I actually liked certain things about Wildwood School. I'm sure it was because of my age. I liked the Mexican boys; I thought they were "cool" because they smoked and cussed. I thought that was big stuff. They seemed rough and tough and that impressed me! Some of the classes were fun. I liked arts and crafts and the music appreciation class because we played music albums and then discussed them. I also enjoyed woodshop.

School was becoming harder and harder for me. I wanted friends, and I was curious about drugs. I regret the bad things I got into while at Wildwood. I got hooked on cigarettes, and I'm still fighting that battle today. I began cussing and getting into trouble; one kid invited me to his house, where I smoked marijuana and thought it was great, so I continued to do so whenever I could.

The kids at Wildwood were allowed to cuss at the teachers and be very disrespectful. Kids also were allowed to smoke.

I know the boys from the boy's home will not have a good life unless they come to know Jesus as their Lord and Savior.

In high school (I was now at the regular high school), I had a really neat teacher. She worked with me and tried to encourage me. She had to quit teaching because she

Todd's Own Story

had a baby. My mom took me to her house to see her and the baby. I understood she couldn't teach any more, but I missed her. The kids that were into drugs seemed "cool" and more accepting of me. I started ditching school and getting into trouble. I was doing drugs and also drinking. I cut classes so much I wasn't able to keep up my grades. At sixteen, the teachers, counselors, and even the nurse met with me to tell me I was being removed from school. They were all so nice and sorry I had to be dropped from school.

They were even tearful, and so was I. I apologized to them because they had all tried to help me, but I wanted to be "cool."

After I left high school, my dad would take me downtown. I was supposed to look for a job. My first job was washing dishes in a restaurant in town. The owner was a real nice lady. Besides being slow, I am also a perfectionist. I tried to clean all the black off the pots and pans. Though she told me I wasn't supposed to get the black off, I still thought I should. My boss said she was sorry to have to let me go, that she knew I was working really hard, but she couldn't let me stay and scrub pans because if I got hurt, she would be in trouble with her insurance. I was never able to hold a job very long because of my slow reactions and wanting to make things perfect. I continued to get into trouble and eventually ended up in jail a couple of times.

Now I started doing real strange things. I took off with a group called "The White Sheets." The leader of the White

Sheets was a man who called himself, "The Lightning Amen." His followers believed he was Jesus, who was back in a flesh body. They believed in three "keys," one, no killing, two, no sex, and three, no materialism.

I went with them because I believed they had the truth. I invited them up to my house to tell my family I was going with them, and I wanted them to believe them, too. My mom and sister tried to talk to them and tried to convince me not to go, but I went with them anyway. I had to throw away my brand-new shoes because they were made of leather. My newfound religion wouldn't allow me to wear anything made from animals. We traveled by foot (barefoot), walking on gravel and broken glass and stickers.

One guy had a truck, and we rode with him once. We also hopped trains. We traveled until we would meet up with what they referred to as the "Christ family." We would go around the towns talking to people, trying to convert them. We were like transients, because we looked in dumpsters for food and would also ask people for food and money. We were not allowed to eat any meat or meat product, not even honey.

When we had traveled as far as Texas, they got tired of waiting on me in the mornings, so they dropped me off at Victory Outreach. I was devastated, I even cried!

One of the leaders at Victory Outreach came over and comforted me. I stayed there for two or three weeks.

A couple guys who were also staying at Victory

Todd's Own Story

Outreach decided to leave, so I went with them. They hopped a train, but I dropped my bed roll and missed the train, so I started hitch-hiking. A truck driver picked me up and took me to his house. I had dinner and spent the night there. The next morning, he took me to a place to eat, bought my breakfast, and gave me $4.00, and I was back hitch hiking again. I was really scared. I was praying to God, and a car stopped to pick me up. It was a guy that said he never picked up hitchhikers, but God told him to stop and pick me up. He played Christian music all the way to Yucaipa. I called my parents to see if I could come home, and they said, "Yes." Dad and Mom said they would come and get me, but the guy said he would bring me home. He took me all the way to my house. My mom wanted to thank him, but he just dropped me off and left. Mom said she believed he was my guardian angel. Even if he wasn't, I know God sent him.

    Just a few years ago, my SSI was stopped, and the social security office said I needed to go to the police station to find out why, that it had something to do with an arrest warrant! My mom and I thought it was a mistake because I hadn't been in trouble for many years. Come to find out, the last time I was released from jail, I didn't finish probation period. They immediately arrested me, and I had to go back to jail. It was hard to imagine, all these years (in my late thirties, then) could go by and the probation department didn't notice my warrant years before. Mom and I were sad and sorry I had to go back to jail when I hadn't done anything since my teen years. Just take note; we reap what we sow, even if it takes a long time to come about. I'm very glad I have finally paid my debt to society.

Mom wanted me to talk about my feelings when I was a teenager toward each of our family members: Dad, Mom, Jill, and Trent. I just couldn't express those feelings because they were so difficult to think about. I realized those negative feelings were from a young person's perspective and not accurate. But when I was in my teens, I thought everyone was against me, especially my family. I know now they were not.

If you are a teen and you are reading this book, please realize when you get older you will understand better that your family and other adults are really trying to help you.

They actually do care and want the best for you. They may not be going about it in the best or even the right way. I think my mom and dad made a lot of mistakes. Mom told me one time, she and Dad kind of learned from me how to be parents since I was the oldest.

My advice to adopted kids is really the same as to any kid. The most important thing is to stay close to God because He will never leave you or forsake you. I hope my story is proof of that. I think it can be harder for adopted kids like me to accept people's love, I guess it is because we think something must be wrong with us if our natural parents would not keep us. That is something else that is

Todd's Own Story

understood better as we get older.

We can actually be grateful for our natural parents caring enough to give us life, and a father, mother, and a family to love us. Many babies are not given that care nowadays. Some are kept by mothers who cannot provide for them. Some may have both parents but do not provide a decent home because of alcohol and/or drugs. Many of them are terminated before they get a chance at life.

I was depressed because I knew I needed to be out of my parent's house. I was thirty-four years old and still at home. I was not eating properly, and I barricaded myself in my bedroom and only came out to go to the bathroom and eat occasionally. I really didn't care if I lived or died. In fact, I thought of committing suicide many times, but I was afraid I'd go to Hell, and I knew that would be worse.

My mom called social workers to come out and try to help me. Two ladies came out, but I locked myself in the bathroom and would not come out, even when they told me they would call the police if I didn't. Our neighbor was the sheriff, and he came over, and I came out for him. He took me to Ward B to be examined. I was diagnosed with bi-polar disorder and schizophrenia. It is very important for people to be properly diagnosed so people like me can be given medication to help them live a better life.

When I moved away from home for good, it was very hard. I know now it was the best for me because at home I was so depressed. I go to counseling that helps me understand myself and others better. I am more able to accept who I am and what I am able to do.

Now I am thankful I was forced to leave home. I was sent to Burley's Board and Care facility where I live today. I have been there thirteen years.

Leaving home for good made me sad. I actually cried when no one was looking. I have adjusted and feel at home at Mrs. Burley's. She is very strict and very loving. She may seem mean when she is in a bad mood, but I think it is when she is not feeling well. She is really a good person, and I love her and appreciate her and all she has done for me. I also realize she has to be strict in order to run a board and care for men.

The policy at Burley's Board and Care is that all the men are to be gone during the day to some kind of facility to engage in some kind of activity that provides counseling and an opportunity to learn certain skills. The first place I was assigned was a government facility called Team House. I was kind of alone and felt no one really cared about me. Then God brought this lady, Cindy, into my life. She was also attending Team House. Cindy lives at a board and care facility for women.

\She is special to me. I think she is cute; she is nice, sweet, loving, and polite.

We have been dating for ten years. Cindy and I have several things in common; we like the same kinds of movies and music, and I have a pet snake. She and I enjoy

Todd's Own Story

watching him. His name is Charlie; he is a Kenyan Sand Boa. I like that Cindy isn't afraid of snakes.

Cindy and I wanted to get married, and I did ask her parents for her hand in marriage, but her parents believed she was not physically able to be married because she was ill quite often. I got along really well with Cindy's parents. They told my parents that they loved me and were sorry we could not marry. Her parents and my parents got along well with each other.

Cindy and I do love each other, and we are just happy to be together whenever possible. My parents take us to church on Sundays. Cindy and I are together a couple other days during the week. Her parents also take us out to eat occasionally.

Cindy and I enjoy going to church to worship God. I love attending church and worshiping God. I love the music, and our minister is very interesting. Worship helps me want to be a better person, and I'm learning how to better serve Him. I can see Jesus' love in the people there.

I'm speaking now particularly to any young person or parent of a young person. My advice is this: stay close to God. We are His children, and He is our Creator. He loves us, and He helps us to stay out of trouble when we listen to His Spirit.

Miraculously My Own

Dear God,

*It's good to be back on track with You.
I'm still not doing everything
I should be doing, but I realize
You are not finished with me yet.*

Thank You,

*In Jesus name,
Amen.*

Chapter 17

PEACE AT LAST

"For He Himself is our peace"

— Ephesians 2: 14a, NASB

I was gazing into the fireplace one evening and desperately prayed, "Father, please, I have to have wisdom to help Todd and bring peace to our family." Still living at home, trouble popped up from time to time though Todd was in his thirties. The following is the answer I received from the Lord: *"... the mind controlled by the Spirit is life and peace"* (Rom. 8:6b, NIV). Rom. 14: 17b (NIV) told me that the kingdom of God is *"...righteousness, peace and joy, in the Holy Spirit!"*

Larry and I were becoming more open to the Spirit's leading. When Jesus baptizes *with the Spirit,* that empowers us to hear the Spirit as He guides us step by step on our spiritual journey. Matt. 3:11, Mark 1:8, Acts 1: 5, and Luke 11:13 are all scriptures testifying that Jesus baptizes us with the Spirit, and all we have to do is ask.

I'm amazed I never saw these scriptures. Well, I saw them, but I never realized that they meant what they said. Growing up in a Christian belief system that did not understand the workings of the Spirit blinded me to the reality of these scriptures.

As I continue to receive the fullness of that gift, the enthusiasm for life has increased more and more. In my desire to serve humanity, I need the power and anointing from the Spirit. I am excited about life and I stand in awe of God's Spirit as He guides me in my journey through this life.

An example of the Holy Spirit's leading is the writing of this book. I thought I had everything ready to publish when God showed me something else, I needed to do.

In a miraculous way God arranged for me to attend the Writer's Gallery in town. This is what happened.

I was working-out at Curves Gym one afternoon. I seldom ever work out in the afternoon, but I did this day. A young girl kept looking at me. She came over to me and asked, "Are you Mrs. Lacey?"

I answered, "Yes."

Then she said, "I am the youngest Hubert girl, I went to church with you several years ago."

I responded, "You must be Sandy, how is everyone in your family doing? How is Diane?"

"They're fine. Diane just opened a Writers Gallery in town."

I said, "Really? I have just written a book!"

"You should go see her."

I said, "Yes, I will," and I did that day.

For more than a year now, I have attended the gallery,

having my work critiqued by these wonderfully capable people. However, I have never seen Sandy at the gym again.

Some people would call that a coincidence. But I know it was inspired by the Spirit. This is just one example of His leading. Time after time He has intervened from the beginning of this book project and continues to lead and guide me. I'm sure that is so I do not get ahead of God and His perfect timing, and I will learn to trust Him.

Another thing Larry and I decided to do was to ask God where He wanted us to go to worship Him. He guided us to a church where we could develop our talents and grow spirituality. Now we are learning how to receive the promised abundant life as we worship together in church. When sadness or tragedy comes our way, His body, the church, gives us the support we need. I can't imagine life without the love and fellowship of our church family. Isaiah 54: 13 (KJV) says, *"All thy children shall be taught of the Lord and great shall be the peace of thy children."*

Now I had the answer to my prayer: listen to the Spirit, love God, obey His Word, and teach my children to do the same.

In John 14: 27 (NASB), Jesus said He was giving us *His peace, not the kind of peace the world gives, so don't be afraid.* We are so grateful that we cannot help but rejoice in all the Lord is doing for us.

Though we have lots to learn yet, we're so blessed to

have found *the key* to our family's peace: *The Holy Spirit*, who lives inside us and comforts and guides us in all our ways.

The Spirit taught Larry and me to accept Todd as he is: a precious gift from God. Through his very challenging life, we learned to unconditionally love our family and others also. This love began the healing process that our family needed.

Larry's and my journey over these sixty plus years has been with many mountains and valleys, as is everyone's. Ours may have had deeper valleys than some, but I'm aware they were not as deep as many sojourners in this world.

What have I learned? I learned I have an incredible husband who stuck by me through all the valleys, when many men would have left. I learned God gave Larry and me three wonderful gifts: Todd, our precious, adorable, destiny and longed-for-child of many years; Jill, my compassionate, intelligent, talented, and beautiful daughter; and Trent my good-looking, smart, funny, and loving son.

God had added Todd's girlfriend, Cindy. Like Todd, she lived in a board and care facility. They met about thirteen years ago at a government run facility that helped give adults an opportunity to develop any skills they might have. Cindy was a sweet, loving, polite, and sensitive girl, and we loved her very much. We felt blessed to have come to know her. Sadly, two years later, she went to be with the

PEACE AT LAST

Lord, I'm praying that Todd will be able to continue to find peace; without her, he is very sad and depressed.

Jill blessed our family with her very attractive husband, Mick. He is a kind, gentle Christian man, and a wonderful father. There are two grandsons: Shane, twenty years old, a handsome, quick minded, and loving young man, and sixteen year-old Preston, my good-looking, smart, game competitor.

Trent added three blessings also. His wife, Jackie, I could have searched the world over and never found a daughter-in-law more perfect. Jackie is beautiful, a great wife, and mother, so precious, loving, and considerate of Larry and me. Trent and Jackie blessed us with a grandson, Peyton. He is now twelve years old, cute as could be, brown eyed, ball of fire, and smart as a whip. A daughter Vivian, who is now seven years old and is my longed for, adorable, tender hearted, and entertaining granddaughter.

I first started writing this book several years ago; I am now bringing it more up to date. Shane, Jill and Mick's oldest son, is now twenty-nine and married to a precious girl, Amber, and they have three boys, Jadon, Caleb, and Noah. Preston is now age twenty-six and working with a mission group.

Trent and Jackie's son Peyton now age twenty and in his first year of collage at Cal Poly. Their daughter Vivian is in her second year of high school.

Larry and I found the baptism with the Holy Spirit was the missing piece that brought our peace picture into view. I'm sure we will be working on the "Perfect Peace Puzzle" until Jesus comes. However, we have put enough pieces together that we are able to see the picture of love and respect for one another taking shape. Only our God could have accomplished this in and for our family. Besides that, He promised that,

One day our Prince Jesus will come...

Why is it that in every human heart, after overcoming the evil in their life, has a desire to be rescued by a wonderful, trustworthy person (prince) and be safe and secure forever? Fairy tales express that overwhelming desire. Therefore, though we think of them as fantasy, they actually tell the truth about the future of good over evil.

One day, our Prince will come *riding on a white horse* (Revelations 19:11)! He promises to take us to live with Him in His majestic home in heaven. Then we, as all fairy tales predict, will truly *live happily ever after* with Him, our *Prince of peace,* Jesus!

John 14:3 (NASB) says, *"I go to prepare a place for you; I will come again, and receive you unto Myself; that where I am, there you may be also."*

PEACE AT LAST

THOU WILL KEEP HIM IN PERFECT PEACE WHOSE MIND IS STAYED ON THEE.

--Isaiah 26:3, KJV

I Praise You Father,

For Your wisdom that helps Larry and me better understand Your wonderful and marvelous love. Your Spirit has brought us to a close and personal relationship with Jesus, our "Prince of Peace." Help us to keep our thoughts pure and our hearts tender so we will continue to receive the peace that only You can give.

In Jesus' name,
Amen

Epilogue

It's been a while since I finished writing this book, so I needed to update you on what has been going on in Todd's life since Cindy died.

A strange thing happened in their relationship before she died. Cindy had emphysema, and several times had to be admitted to the hospital with pneumonia. We took Todd to visit each time. Todd had been attending a counselling group while Cindy had been in the hospital that was to help him with his mental and emotional problems. The last time Cindy got out of the hospital; Todd told Cindy that he met a girl. Sometimes, Todd would say what he thought and wouldn't think about what he was saying, so he said to Cindy, *"I met a girl in group, and I think I like her more than you."* Of course, after fifteen years, she was devastated.

Todd was so sorry and tried to make it up to her. He wrote letters, called her, and she would not respond in any way. Crying, he would call me, and he even called Cindy's mom and she would just say, "So sorry Todd, but it's up to Cindy."

This is my opinion about the situation. I believe that Cindy knew that she did not have long to live, and she loved Todd so much that she did not want him to have to be with her during the last days of her life. That she wanted him to remember her as she was and not having to remember her as she was dying.

Todd was very depressed, and though we found him a very nice board and care home, he didn't like the strict rules there, depressing him more. So, one day, he called the police on himself as he said he felt suicidal, and they took him to the hospital's psychiatric ward. While he was there, he met some guys that told him he could live where they lived for only $700.00 a month, and they would move him right in. So, they took Todd to where he lived, packed him up, and moved him in with them.

This was the first time Todd had ever moved without consulting us. We found out later, most of the people there were on drugs. These were hard drugs. So, it wasn't long till we noticed Todd was not acting right. This place moved him again to a place of theirs in Mentone. Todd thought we would be happy because it was closer to us.

But come to find out, that place was even worse. Even the manager was on drugs.

Todd got so bad we had to take him to the hospital and get him out of that place. Todd still wanted to go to a room and board place because it was cheaper. So, we found him a supposed Christian place. They did the best they could, but Todd wasn't happy there because there was too much turmoil and fighting among the men, and he was feeling suicidal again. So, as he did before, he called the police on himself, and they took him to the hospital psychiatric ward.

Epilogue

I was glad he called for help each time.

This time, the hospital helped find him a board and care place that has been very successful, though it costs him more. He likes the food, and these are older people that have not necessarily been in trouble, so there is not quite as much turmoil there. Though it sometimes gets loud, Todd says. The place is very clean, and they even let him have a snake as a pet. It is my constant prayer that he will be stay there for the rest of his life and be content and receive the peace and comfort that only the Holy Spirit can provide.

Todd really misses Cindy so much, but he knows she is now well, happy, and that he will see her again one day, and they will both be well and live happily ever after.

Dear Father,

Thank You so much for Your grace and mercy.
Help Todd receive Your love.
Help him know that You are all he needs
until You come, or he comes to You.

In Jesus Name,
Amen

Our 50th

Wedding Anniversary Celebration

August 26th 2007

On the Icon YachtMNew Port Beach, Ca.

A Gift from our Children

Collection of Pictures from our 50th Wedding Anniversary

Todd and his girlfriend, Cindy, at the anniversary celebration on the yacht.

Todd and Cindy at the anniversary reception.

Miraculously My Own

Todd, Trent, Me, Larry, and Jill on the Yacht.

Entire anniversary party.

Family Picture with Joyce's Necie Patti Jo (Todd, Jill, Patti Jo, Joyce, Larry and Trent)

Prayer book like I carried on our original wedding day.

CPSIA information can be obtained
at www.ICGtesting.com
Printed in the USA
LVHW072131040322
712646LV00028B/2791